CW00350459

PRAISE
RAISE YOUR VIBRATION
AND
KYLE GRAY

"Kyle certainly knows how to live a high-vibe life and this book is filled with inspiration so you can do exactly that!"

VEX KING, BEST-SELLING AUTHOR OF *GOOD VIBES, GOOD LIFE* AND *HEALING IS THE NEW HIGH*

"Kyle Gray is a... guide for a new generation of spiritual seekers and the already converted."

GABRIELLE BERNSTEIN, BEST-SELLING AUTHOR OF *SUPER ATTRACTOR* AND *THE UNIVERSE HAS YOUR BACK*

"I adore Kyle Gray. He helps you to reconnect with all that is wanting to rise up within you, be available to the benevolent support that already surrounds you and release what is wanting to fall away with grace and ease. Who doesn't want some of that?!"

REBECCA CAMPBELL, AUTHOR OF *LIGHT IS THE NEW BLACK* AND *WORK YOUR LIGHT ORACLE*

"Kyle Gray is now an expert on celestial connections and has the following to prove it."

YOU MAGAZINE

"Kyle represents the future of spiritual wellbeing; he is both deeply insightful and wildly relatable. He gives me faith that we are in good hands for the future generations of seekers and spiritual practitioners, all while rocking a fresh pair of Jordans."

MICHAEL JAMES WONG, BEST-SELLING AUTHOR OF
SENBAZURU AND FOUNDER OF JUST BREATHE

"Kyle Gray... has a remarkable spiritual connection."

DAVID R. HAMILTON PH.D. AUTHOR OF *WHY WOO-WOO WORKS* AND *HOW YOUR MIND CAN HEAL YOUR BODY*

"I had full-bodied chills. Kyle Gray is the hottest, hippest medium who translates the wisdom of the angels in the most loving and relatable way possible. I couldn't recommend his brilliant spiritual gifts more."

MEGGAN WATTERSON, AUTHOR OF *MARY MAGDALENE REVEALED* AND *HOW TO LOVE YOURSELF (AND SOMETIMES OTHER PEOPLE)*

"Kyle Gray is one of the world's most incredibly gifted angel communicators. I have seen him work and he is authentic, intelligent, and deeply compassionate. I highly recommend him and all his creations."

COLETTE BARON-REID, INTERNATIONAL BEST-SELLING ORACLE EXPERT

"The hottest name in spirituality!"

SOUL & SPIRIT MAGAZINE

RAISE YOUR
VIBRATION

NEW EDITION

ALSO BY KYLE GRAY

BOOKS

Divine Masters, Ancient Wisdom
Angel Numbers
Angel Prayers
Connecting with the Angels Made Easy
Wings of Forgiveness
Angels Whisper in My Ear

AUDIOBOOKS

Raise Your Vibration (New Edition)
Angel Prayers
Angel Prayer Meditations

ORACLE CARD DECKS

Gateway of Light Activation Oracle
The Angel Guide Oracle
Angels and Ancestors Oracle Cards
Keepers of the Light Oracle Cards
Angel Prayers Oracle Cards

ONLINE COURSES

Certified Angel Guide
Connecting with the Angels Made Easy

RAISE YOUR VIBRATION

HIGH-VIBE TOOLS TO SUPPORT YOUR SPIRITUAL AWAKENING

NEW EDITION

KYLE GRAY

HAY HOUSE

Carlsbad, California • New York City
London • Sydney • New Delhi

Published in the United Kingdom by:
Hay House UK Ltd, The Sixth Floor, Watson House,
54 Baker Street, London W1U 7BU
Tel: +44 (0)20 3927 7290; Fax: +44 (0)20 3927 7291; www.hayhouse.co.uk

Published in the United States of America by:
Hay House Inc., PO Box 5100, Carlsbad, CA 92018-5100
Tel: (1) 760 431 7695 or (800) 654 5126
Fax: (1) 760 431 6948 or (800) 650 5115; www.hayhouse.com

Published in Australia by:
Hay House Australia Ltd, 18/36 Ralph St, Alexandria NSW 2015
Tel: (61) 2 9669 4299; Fax: (61) 2 9669 4144; www.hayhouse.com.au

Published in India by:
Hay House Publishers India, Muskaan Complex, Plot No.3, B-2,
Vasant Kunj, New Delhi 110 070
Tel: (91) 11 4176 1620; Fax: (91) 11 4176 1630; www.hayhouse.co.in

A catalogue record for this book is available from the British Library.

Tradepaper ISBN: 978-1-78817-725-2
E-book ISBN:978-1-78817-730-6
Audiobook ISBN: 978-1-78817-726-9

Interior images: p.26, 27, 262: Lucy Webster; p.59, 77, 95, 113, 131, 149, 167, 185, 203, 217, 231, 245, 264: Ari Wisner; p.267: Bob Rafferty

Printed and bound in Great Britain by
TJ Books Ltd, Padstow, Cornwall

CONTENTS

INTRODUCTION

I remember being surprised when I had the publicity meeting for the first edition of this book. It was proving difficult to market. It wasn't that my publisher didn't believe in it, it was more that magazines, newspapers, and other media found it "different" in a direction that they weren't sure they could promote or support. Most of them asked us to rethink and "come back."

It was only a matter of weeks before the book was released and it was already printed.

I remember telling my mother there just wasn't an interest in the book in the larger market. I remember thinking, *I'm going to have to do things differently*. But I believed in the book and its message so much.

"This is my life's work," I said to myself.

After taking some time to meditate on the energy of the book, I realized I needed to take a higher approach. I needed to raise *my* vibration and not get pulled into the details. I needed to surrender.

Right there and then I dropped into prayer. I asked the Universe to take control.

Specifically, I set the clear intention that I was handing the entire project over to my higher power. I visualized the book supporting those who read it. I knew it wasn't about impressing, but about blessing. I trusted it would bless those who were open to it.

After that, every time we worked on the marketing, I would say, "The Universe is handling the finer details," and I really believed it.

I am honored to share that it worked. *Raise Your Vibration* has now sold over 100,000 copies worldwide and has been translated into many languages. It has been the most successful book I've ever written and it continues to reach many.

In the summer of 2019, when I was in New York for a conference, I was in a fashion store treating myself to a new jacket. While I was paying, I got talking to the sales assistant. He asked what had brought me to the city and I explained I was there on business. Before you know it, he was asking what I did.

"I'm an author."

"What kind of material do you write?"

"I write books in the field of spirituality—angels, energy, intuition, that kind of thing."

At that point one of his co-workers came over and said, "Sorry, what did you say your name was?"

"Kyle Gray."

His jaw dropped and he started to fill up.

"Sorry, I'm so shocked I am meeting you right now. Your book *Raise Your Vibration* saved me in one of the hardest and darkest times of my life. I did not want to be on this planet and your work gave me a reason to live."

He came out from behind the till and hugged me. I was blown away.

Right there, in that moment, in a city far from home, I was reminded of the importance of this work. It's not about getting press or being marketable, it's about changing lives and supporting healing.

I remember leaving the store and walking up Greene Street in Soho with my sunglasses steaming up from tears of joy evaporating in the midday sun.

Thank you, Universe!

Since the initial publication of *Raise Your Vibration*, living a high-vibe life has become a bit of a trend. Many of us are feeling called to live in a more conscious and heart-centered way. It's evident from some of the things happening in the world that it's needed—we need folks to become more mindful, more positive, and more supportive of themselves, those around them, and ultimately the planet.

We are recognizing that we have the ability to change the vibe of a conversation, space, or even relationship just through how we express ourselves. That is huge. It's a recognition of our responsibility, and the fact that you are here with this book in your hand right now means that you've made a conscious choice to be someone who makes a difference.

That's what raising your vibration is all about—it's about choosing to be that good vibe wherever you go. Essentially, it's about making the conscious choice to be the good you were born to be.

So, before we dive into how you can be that good vibe, I want to thank you for being here.

Thank you from me.

Thank you from humanity.

The high-vibe life is a good life. That doesn't mean that everything's going to be rosy, but it does mean that you have tools and practices that you can use when you need them.

That's what I've learned about raising your vibration—it's not about avoiding life's challenges or high-vibing your way out of being human, it's about being able to come back to your center more quickly when things get gnarly, challenging, or even dark.

My prayer is that no matter what comes up in your life, this book will support you in tapping into the resources you have within and returning to the highest vibration.

EVERYTHING IS ENERGY

*"Energy cannot be destroyed; it can only be
changed from one form to another."*

ALBERT EINSTEIN

There's one thing that psychics and scientists can agree on:
everything in the Universe is made up of energy. That includes you.
Right now, energy is moving through every cell of your body and
every atom of the air you are breathing.

And that energy is alive.

That means it moves. It vibrates. It vibrates so intensely that we
cannot see it with our human eyes, but we can feel it, and it helps us
"read" the environments we're in and the people we're exposed to.

You may not even realize it, but you are constantly responding to
the energy around you. You know what it's like to walk into a room
and be met with a "bad vibe," don't you? Or to feel the "good vibe"
when a friend you haven't seen in forever is walking toward you
with a big smile on their face.

We don't just receive energy, we transmit it too. We've all been
the person who has got out of the wrong side of the bed and isn't
fun to be around, and we've all been the person who is living their

best life and is great to be with. We all transmit energy through our actions, non-actions, thoughts, and feelings.

But that's not all. Think for a moment. What else do we do?

We transform energy.

That's what you do when you make the conscious decision to raise your vibration. So, how does it work?

The Law of Vibration

"Nothing rests; everything moves, everything vibrates."

THE KYBALION

In a spiritual context, the Law of Vibration was introduced to the modern world through the 1908 book *The Kybalion*. This is a set of Hermetic principles, teachings that were shared by masters of ancient Egypt and Greek philosophy, that can help us understand the spiritual workings of the Universe today. Its authors were "three initiates," which was most likely a pseudonym for William Walker Atkinson, a popular new thought writer of the time.

The Kybalion shares:

"Every thought, emotion or mental state has its corresponding rate and mode of vibration. And by the effort of the will of the person, or of other persons, these mental states may be reproduced, just as a musical tone may be reproduced by causing an instrument to vibrate at a certain rate—just as color may be reproduced in the same way. By a

*knowledge of the principle of vibration, as applied
to mental phenomena, one may polarize his mind
at any degree he wishes, thus gaining perfect
control over his mental states and moods."*

So, everything in the entire Universe is in motion, including our thoughts and feelings. A thought is like a ripple when we drop a pebble into water—it moves away from us, creating changes in the field around us. And, just as a ripple moves out and comes back on a wave, our thoughts come back to us. For that reason, when we change our thoughts, we change our world.

I first heard about this through Louise Hay. She was one of the first spiritual authors I read and I instantly fell in love with her. In her life-changing work Louise helps us realize that we can choose to think loving thoughts or be stuck in fear. Essentially, it's our choice, but we know that one is going to be better than the other.

The miracle lies in our capacity to change the way we think—change our energy, change our vibration. Then the Universe will respond accordingly.

The Universe

When I talk about the Universe, I'm talking about the Source of creation. But this Source isn't like our human ideas about God, it's an intelligent force that we're not only connected to but part of. It isn't a governing body, but an intelligence that is constantly responding to other forms of vibration, including us.

The Universe is responding to our vibration even when we don't realize it. Most of the time we don't realize that we get to choose what sort of energy we give off, receive, and surround ourselves with. Or that our feelings are usually making the choice for us. For example, if you're going around feeling like a failure, then failure is going to be your story. If you're going around feeling contented, even with small things, then you'll continue along that pathway.

The Universe is unlimited and has so much to offer us, but we live in a world of limitations. It sounds crazy when you think about it, but we're led to believe that we can't have what we want and even that we can lose everything we do have. That's nothing but an *illusion*.

Energy is unlimited and never-ending—it will never cease to be. We are all part of the oneness of life, and even when our body dies, our energy will continue to live on. We will just move from the physical to the non-physical. Does that feel like a loss? It's not a loss, it's simply moving back to our natural state of being.

The point is that when we accept that we are limitless, we allow limitless possibilities into our life. Including miracles.

Miracles

Most of us think of a miracle as a "Wow!" event like surviving a near-death experience, being healed from a life-threatening illness, or even being visited by a holy figure, but the metaphysical text *A Course in Miracles* defines a miracle simply as "a shift in perception." So:

- A miracle is choosing to forgive rather than argue.

- A miracle is healing from a wound.

- A miracle is having a roof over your head and a family to love.

- A miracle is waking up each morning.

4

I really like this way of thinking, but it can take a moment to get your head and heart around it, for we have been brought up in a world that gives some things a greater value than others. This measuring system can even seep into our own self-worth and block our experience of miracles.

In order to open up to the miraculous, we need to stop seeing some things as more miraculous than others.

According to *A Course in Miracles*:

> **"There is no order of difficulty in miracles.**
>
> **One is not 'harder' or 'bigger' than another.**
>
> **They are all the same."**

All miracles are miracles. So don't let your ego limit you. *Every* miracle is possible. If you are making the miracle you need "too big" to achieve, it never will be achievable, but if you can believe that it is destined to happen because all miracles are possible, then there's a greater chance of experiencing it.

Every single day, normal people are achieving the unachievable.

Every single day, normal people are experiencing miracles.

> **Miracles are yours to have.**
>
> **You just need to raise your vibration to match theirs and you'll experience them tenfold.**

The Universe is limitless, remember—it will never stop giving. But so often we live in a false reality, believing that energy is running out or that there are more deserving cases out there. But experiencing a miracle isn't depriving anyone else of experiencing a miracle. Hoping for a miracle isn't self-importance or narcissism. Receiving a miracle shows others they can receive them too.

A Course in Miracles says:

> *"Miracles are not in competition, and the number of them that you can do is limitless."*

So, take a moment to answer these questions:

- What miracle do you need?

- Is this miracle something that you have made "huge" in your mind, so huge that you think it might not be possible?

- If so, are you willing to change your perception?

When you change your perception, you change your frequency, and that ripples out into the field of creation and supports the miraculous unfolding of your life.

You deserve miracles simply because you exist. As far as I'm concerned, we are all miracles in the first place and we can all create them. We can all change the way we think and bring about a change in our life. It doesn't have to be a dramatic outer event— it can be a subtle inner shift that creates a feeling of richness and wholeness.

Here's a thought that has helped me. It's from my journal:

> *"It's not how big the miracle is, it's how much room you make for it."*

When you raise your vibration, you make room for miracles. You prepare the space inside yourself to receive love and support from the Universe. And when you create a daily spiritual practice, which we'll look at later, you take the time to remind yourself that you deserve miracles.

For now, welcome miracles into your life with this prayer:

> *"Today I realize that my life and world*
> *are surrounded by miracles.*
>
> *Miracles are part of my everyday life.*
>
> *I don't wish for miracles, I expect them,*
> *for when miracles occur, nature is*
> *unfolding as it intended.*
>
> *I believe in miracles because I am a miracle.*
>
> *Miracles are attracted to my vibration.*
>
> *I give thanks for the miracle of life*
> *and the miracle of love.*
>
> *And so it is."*

THE UNIVERSE IS RECRUITING YOU

"Spiritual advancement is not measured by one's outward powers, but only by the depth of one's bliss in meditation."

PARAMAHANSA YOGANANDA

It's not a mistake that you're here now. You have been called by the Universe—the Source of infinite creation.

Before you were in this life, you danced among the stars. You were part of the cosmos. Today, your human body is made up of carbon, therefore you are made up of the particles of former stars.

You are a star in its next form.

Wanting to raise your vibration is ultimately a soul-led desire to remember who you are. It's answering a call—a call to remember, a call to be more, a call to lead a better, more heart-centered life.

The Universe itself has sent that call. It has sent signs.

9

The true meaning of signs

You may have received several signs from the Universe—signs sent to let you know that there is a large-scale, light-fueled operation going on upon this planet, and you are being called to be part of it.

If you get an inkling that you are receiving a sign, you are. In that moment, you are being given three important messages:

You are on the right path

Whenever you receive a sign, the ultimate message is that you are on the right path. I'll tell you why—signs only show up when you are in alignment. So, when your energy is consciously connected to the Universe and you are making choices that are aligned with your highest good, signs will undoubtedly show up.

You are not alone

Receiving a sign is also a message that you are not alone. Angels, spiritual guides, and ancestors are with you. All of life is supporting your evolution.

Help is available

When you receive a sign, you are aligned with wisdom, guidance, insight, and awareness, and for that reason you have access to direct downloads of information.

So, whenever you receive a sign, take the opportunity to receive support. Whatever you're working on, working through, healing or manifesting, a sign is saying there's support available, and all you need to do is ask.

Just close your eyes (if that's practical), amp up your breathing, and say a prayer:

> *"Thank you, Universe, for revealing to me*
> *what I need to know. I am willing to receive.*
> *I am willing to listen. And so it is."*

Even if you don't receive direct information, the fact you took a moment to pause will create the magic, and the "downloads" will show up later as inspiration, creativity, or even in a dream.

So that's what signs ultimately mean, but how do they show up?

11:11

Have you ever seen repetitive numbers on your clock, phone, or even a receipt from the store? Numbers like 1:11, 2:22, 3:33? Personally, I've seen them everywhere.

It's become a bit of a trend to make a wish when you see 11:11, and I trust that the Universe is actually working with that. But, as someone who really likes to get their own information, I dropped into meditation one day to get the answers that Google couldn't supply.

I said, "Thank you, Universe, for helping me understand the true meaning of 11:11 or 111," and the answer came in a vision.

Instantly I saw a golden Buddha on an altar. I saw Muslims praying at Mecca, I saw an image of Christ, an image of pagans dancing round a roaring midsummer fire, images of Bob Marley, Martin Luther King, and people connecting. Then I heard, "We are all one. One. One. One. One."

I came out of the meditation and then it clicked: 11:11 = one, one, one, one.

Seeing 11:11 or 111 is a reminder that we are all one. And because we are all one, everything that we are doing, saying, feeling, experiencing, and choosing is contributing to the whole.

That's why 11:11 isn't just about making a wish, it's a call to action. It's a reminder that you have an opportunity to contribute, to make a difference. You are being called to be a light.

Now when I see 11:11, I say this prayer, which was inspired by *A Course in Miracles*:

"Dear Universe,

Where would you have me go?

Who would you have me speak to?

What would you have me say?

How can I contribute to the healing of the world?

*Thank you for showing me how I can serve
in a way that also serves myself.*

And so it is."

You might like to say this prayer too. And then be open to taking inspired action. Be open to being the highest vibration in the room.

Other number sequences

There are many number patterns and sequences that may appear. In fact I've written a whole book on them, *Angel Numbers*, but here are some that you may see when you're working on raising your vibration.

1234/12:34

I like to call this "the ladder," for it represents moving up the spiritual ladder. You are being told that you are taking the right steps to raise your vibration and make a positive change in the world.

Whenever I see this number sequence, I say, "12:34—it's time to level up, up, up!"

222/22:22

Two is a number of partnership, friendship, and union. If 11:11 is about oneness, 22:22/222 is about bringing that oneness together. It's a divine call to recognize that your intentions and actions have an effect upon others. Therefore, it's inviting you to give a high-vibrational experience to those around you. Not only those you love—you want to reach out to those who are your greatest challenges too.

333/3:33

Thirty-three is an auspicious number in spirituality, because it is believed that Jesus lived to this age. In numerology it is known as the "Master Teacher" number. For this reason, it has become strongly associated with the ascended masters, who are spiritual teachers and change agents who once walked the Earth but now offer their support, based on their life lessons, from the heart of the Universe/heaven.

When 3:33/333 shows up, it's telling you not only that you're a leader of some kind, but also that the great leaders and teachers who have gone before you are encouraging you.

444/4:44

Four is a number of communication and expression. In modern spirituality, 444/4:44 has become known as *the* angel number. Whenever you see it, it's saying that your guardian angels, guides, and loved ones in the spiritual realms are all around you.

One of the keys to experiencing the support of angels is to become more like them, for if you can *be* the angel, you will *see* the angel. So, when you see this sign, ask yourself how you can support, guide, and love unconditionally, just like an angel.

555/5:55

Five is a number of action and change. Usually, it's an invitation from the Universe to be the change you want to see in the world. If there's something that needs to be healed or fixed, what can you do to help? How can you heal this issue in your own life? For whatever you do for yourself is what you are offering to the whole.

I like to see 555 as the number the Universe sends me when I need to take action. It's a gentle kick in the butt.

High-pitched noises

Provided you don't suffer from tinnitus, hearing high whistle-like sounds or high-pitched noises is a sign that you are receiving a high-frequency "download" from the Universe. The way I see it is that we're like walking radios that pick up signals. Often when I'm speaking about something spiritual or about to do spiritual work, I'll hear a high-pitched whistle and I see this as a sign to pause and check in to see what is coming through.

Hearing your name

Hearing your name being called can be a bit freaky. I think we can probably blame horror movies for this. But when your name is called out of the blue, it isn't some weird spirit trying to get your attention, it's the Universe expressing its love for you and calling you to action, because it can see that you have a unique opportunity to offer your light to the world.

What next?

So, you've heard the call, you've received the signs, and the Universe has recruited you. You've been invited to raise your vibration and the vibration of all the people around you. The fact that you're here shows that you've responded to that call and are ready to initiate the process.

The light that is shining within you will now get brighter and brighter and begin to light others up too. In order to progress along this path, it's important to be clear with the Universe, the angels, and your guides that you accept this mission. Don't worry, though—that doesn't mean you have to quit your job or work 24/7 for the spirit world. It just means that you're willing to contribute to the healing and nurturing of the world. You're willing to raise your vibration. You're willing to raise the vibration of the world.

Let's go!

HIGH VIBES IN YOUR BODY

*"What lies behind us and what lies before us are
tiny matters compared to what lies within us."*

ATTRIBUTED TO RALPH WALDO EMERSON

Your physical body is the home of your soul in this incarnation
and the space where your mind dwells. For these reasons alone, it
needs loving care and attention in order to support everything you
are doing, including raising your vibration.

The body–mind connection

The mind and body are connected—the mind has an effect on
the body. Our body displays how we really feel. We know this to
be true based on even some of the most temporary of emotions.
When we feel embarrassed, our face will go red, for example. When
we're nervous, we can have an unsettled tummy. These everyday
moments are often overlooked, but are powerful reminders that
the mind can indeed affect the body.

In fact, every thought we think, every word we speak, and every
emotion we feel has an effect on our physical being. But this isn't a
call for blame or to feel concerned about having negative thoughts
or emotions, more a reminder that every time you have a negative
or challenging thought, it's an opportunity to raise your vibration.

There's a lot of scientific evidence for the body–mind connection. I personally am a huge fan of Louise Hay's work. She was the founder of Hay House Publishing, which she established when she was 60 years young. She had a challenging start in life, which led her on a challenging journey until she discovered the Science of Mind teachings in the second half of her life. Through them, she learned about the power of the mind and she trained as a licensed practitioner within the Science of Mind movement, working with clients to help them fix their lives through affirmations, prayers, and intentions.

It was during Louise's time in the Science of Mind movement that she noticed that certain beliefs or ideas had a correlation with specific dis-eases. Although she didn't say the thoughts *created* the challenges, she did observe that changing them would contribute to the healing.

She went on to create "the little blue book" (now called *Heal Your Body*), which contains a list of physical ailments with their mental-emotional correlations and new thoughts/affirmations to support their healing. This book has now become a must-have for complementary therapists and coaches. It will help you learn what may have caused or contributed to discomfort in your own life— and how you can heal it!

I'll give you an example of how it has helped me personally. I was going through a bit of a funk one time and I kept saying, "I'm so pissed off." I said it for about a week straight and it became a bit of an affirmation. By the end of that week, I was finding it difficult to pee. I went to the doctor and it turned out I had a UTI. When I got home, I checked Louise's book for the mental–emotional correlation, and it said: "Pissed off at life." Isn't that strange? When I was affirming, "I'm pissed off," I was literally turning off my pee.

Our body really is reflecting everything we are thinking, believing, and saying.

Here are three more important pieces of information that will support your healing journey:

Visualization works

The brain cannot tell the difference between visualizing or imagining something and actually doing it. Therefore, when you think healing thoughts, your brain actually accepts healing as a reality.

Stress reduction heals

Scientific tests have proved that reducing stress can help the healing of wounds. The wounds that were studied were physical wounds, but the principle is the same for emotional wounds too.

Loving thoughts are powerful

Sending loving thoughts to people, particularly those you are already in touch with, has been proven to have a mental, emotional, and physical effect on them. Experiments have demonstrated that loving thoughts can support the healing of others.

Uniting with your body

Your body is a wondrous place to be, for it's a unique precious gem. But for some reason, due to the conditioning of the mundane world, we often find ourselves disliking or mistreating our body in ways we don't even realize.

If you don't love your body for some reason, you'll find yourself longing for that love, and often it'll seem more possible when a specific thing happens or changes. But what I've come to understand is that when we love our body anyway, for what it does, we have a far greater capacity to create a better place to be.

In my teenage years I worked professionally doing spiritual readings and I was often out doing them late into the evening. Lifting my energy to read people's vibes and channel angels would make me feel high. Afterward, I would crave the feeling of being grounded or tired, so I could switch off, and I got into the habit of picking up heavy, greasy, sludgy food on the way home. It worked, in the sense that I would feel so heavy I would fall asleep, but was it serving me? Absolutely not.

I was in a pattern I knew wasn't in line with my most authentic self or the raising of my vibration, and I knew my body was becoming overweight. Now, to be clear, I'm not saying that skinnier people have a higher vibration or are more consciously connected. I think it's more about recognizing what we are doing with our body and that that has everything to do with what we are experiencing on a vibrational level.

The high-vibe diet?

If you're like me, you'll have tried a million different health fads and dabbled in changing your diet—keto, vegan, celery juice, organic, kale, kombucha, and the list goes on. Over the years, I've tried them all. Some have felt more supportive, others less. I'm not here to lecture you on diet, but to encourage you to find a way of being that supports you, body and soul.

When you're navigating all this, it's important to be aware of how you feel. If you feel good after eating something, it's likely to be good for you; if you feel heavy or sleepy, it's not supporting your wellness.

When I started to delve into spirituality, I felt the call to become more vegetarian and I went on to eat exclusively "veggie" for around 16 years.

One thing I want to share, though, is that vegetarian/vegan doesn't automatically equal high-vibrational. There's a lot of veggie/vegan food out there that's highly processed, salted, and packed in plastic. It's completely factory-made and barely has the light of day in it, so it isn't going to support the elevation of anyone's vibration. It's important to align your food choices with what you feel is most ethically sustainable and how you want to feel.

I can say from personal experience that eating plant-based food does have a higher vibe. When I eat the rainbow, that is, have fresh foods on my plate that are naturally colorful, I feel alive and inspired.

Food that holds sunlight is food of the light. So foods that have grown in nature, with the help of the sun, will absolutely have pure life-force in them.

When it comes to eating animal products, it's important to know the source. Where did your meat come from? How was the animal reared and treated? For all this is what you are choosing to put into your body.

Where I am now with my diet is completely flexible. I eat whatever is available, though I center around foods I know are holding light. I won't avoid meat or fish, especially if well reared or wild caught.

But whenever I eat, I give thanks, and if it's an animal product, I give thanks to that being too.

I believe a high-vibrational diet is eating in a way that is aware, sustainable, and causes the least harm possible. If you can support local businesses, avoid highly processed, highly salted food, and fill your plate with as much color as possible, you'll absolutely benefit.

Blessing your food

Blessing your food is a wonderful means of lifting the energy of what you're about to consume. There are several ways of doing it. You can visualize it being washed in golden light, you can place your hands over it and visualize light coming from them, or you can just say a prayer, for example:

> *"Thank you, universal life-force, for blessing*
> *this food with unconditional love. I allow*
> *it to nourish every cell of my being!"*

And for the times you forget, you can bless the food in your belly too:

> *"Thank you, Universe, for blessing the food in my*
> *belly. It feels so good to be nourished and well."*

Keeping your body clean and clear

As we've already acknowledged, the body is the temple in which the soul resides, and for that reason it's important to keep it operating at the highest vibration we possibly can. There are a few things that I do regularly for my body that I believe keep it working well and keep my energy clean.

Sea-salt baths

For hundreds of years sea salt has been recognized as a sacred tool to clear away anything that isn't serving us. I like using it in the bath. All you have to do is put a generous amount of sea salt in a nice warm bath. I like to add a few drops of my favorite essential oils too.

Smoothies and juices

I love a green juice or smoothie, because it's an easy way to nourish the body. Putting fresh organic fruit and vegetables together for a refreshing juice is an awesome way to kick-start the day. I believe a healthy gut is important and I've always noticed that having a green juice stimulates my digestive system to release in a healthy way.

Yoga and exercise

Another great way to raise the energy of the body is through yoga and other forms of exercise. I don't know about you, but once I started to exercise regularly in a way that pleased me, I would leave the class or gym feeling high on life. So, if you want to live a high-vibrational lifestyle, it's important to find a regular exercise routine that suits you, your body, and your level of fitness.

"To do" list

In summary, to look after your body and raise your vibes, do the following:

- Check in with your diet and nutrition. Are you eating foods that are making you feel lethargic? How can you improve your eating patterns? Are you eating too much or not enough?

- Begin to bless your food before eating, and if you forget, try blessing the food in your belly instead.

- Add a regular sea-salt bath to your routine. See how it amps up your vibes!

- Try making a green juice or smoothie at home. If you don't know where to start, your local health-food store or juice bar would be a great place to seek inspiration.

- Find a way to exercise that makes your heart sing and your energy soar.

HIGH VIBES IN YOUR SUBTLE BODY

"As one opens the door with a key, so the yogi should open the gate to liberation with the kundalini ... the opening through which one can ascend to that place where there is neither pain nor suffering."

<small>HATHA YOGA PRADĪPIKĀ</small>

When we speak about raising our vibration, we know it's about elevating our frequency on an energetic level, but there's something rising in our subtle body too—our kundalini, our primal spiritual energy!

Welcome to your subtle anatomy lesson [puts on glasses, points to the board]. The following information is commonly accepted in modern spirituality and is highly influenced by the Tantric and Ayurvedic traditions. So, many thanks to the traditions of Mother India for our understanding of the subtle aspects of our being.

The nadis

Nadi is a Sanskrit word meaning "river" or "tunnel," and in this context it refers to a channel of energy. We have numerous nadis, but there are three main ones, known as Ida, Pingala, and Sushumna. Sushumna runs from the base of the spine to the crown of the head, and Ida and Pingala run alongside, carrying femme and masc energies and crossing Sushumna at major points in the endocrine system, creating vortices of energy that are known as chakras (*see below*). *Chakra* is the Sanskrit word for "wheel" or "vortex."

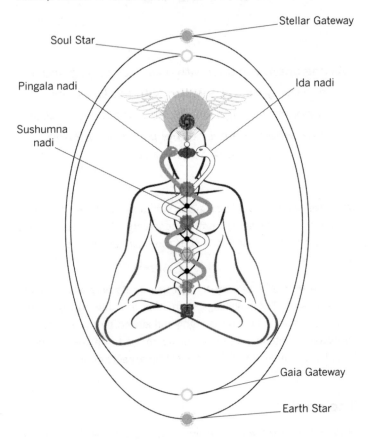

Energy flow in the subtle body

This is depicted in the staff of Hermes, the caduceus, where two serpents dance up a central channel (*see below*). The wings at the top represent the higher states of awareness that are reached when the chakras are actualized.

Interestingly, this is now an internationally recognized symbol of health and healing. You'll find it on ambulances.

The caduceus

The chakras

The traditional chakras

The chakras are the body's spiritual energy centers. According to Tantric teachings and yogic medicine, there are seven main chakras, six of which are created by the movement of energy through Ida and Pingala. The seventh is an effect of the Sushumna channel coming into alignment. These traditional chakras are:

- *The root chakra:* This chakra is the most important, because in most things we have to start from the ground up. Found at the base of the spine, it is all about our security and survival, but it also governs the health of our legs and back.

- *The sacral chakra:* Found just below the navel at the tip of the pubic bone, this chakra governs the reproductive system. It is about our ability to flow with life and express our creativity.

- *The solar plexus chakra:* Lying around the center of the belly, this chakra is our "gut instinct," the brain of the body. It governs the digestive system and is all about our willpower and ability to achieve.

- *The heart chakra:* Located at the center of the chest, this chakra is all about our capacity to give and receive—it's about love, generosity, and sharing a loving experience. It looks after the heart and upper respiratory system too.

- *The throat chakra:* Our ability to communicate is governed by this chakra. Not only does it help us speak our truth, but also express ourselves on an emotional level. It also looks after the thyroid gland, which governs our hormonal stability.

- *The brow chakra (the third eye):* This chakra is concerned with our ability to perceive, on both a physical and non-physical level. It looks after our physical eyes, but helps us develop our inner vision too.

- *The crown chakra:* This is the most elevated of the traditional chakras. Some say it's at the crown of the head, while others say it's just above it. It governs our wisdom and our connection to the divine.

The "higher" chakras

Many people walking the spiritual pathway have heard of the seven traditional chakras, but "higher" chakras are now being rediscovered.

I used to work with three of these, but since the first edition of this book another one, the Gaia Gateway (*see page 217*), has come to my awareness, so I now work with four:

- ◆ Earth Star
- ◆ Soul Star
- ◆ Gaia Gateway
- ◆ Stellar Gateway

Two of these, the Earth Star and Gaia Gateway, are below the feet and the other two, the Soul Star and Stellar Gateway, are above the crown.

The best way to describe the higher chakras is as portals, for they are energetic gateways between the physical body and the higher dimensions. They can be accessed once the kundalini has risen through the seven chakras of the body and they can help us access the hidden knowledge of both heaven and Earth and create a high-vibrational way of life that will ultimately be heaven on Earth.

Chakra alignment

All of the chakras are said to be like spinning wheels. I've always imagined them as little stargate portals swirling with energy. Through highly emotional or challenging moments, or physical challenges, some of these centers can have too much energy and others can become depleted. The goal is to bring them into what some call "balance," but is better described as "alignment."

If all our chakras are in alignment, they create a clear channel for the kundalini to rise up, which then permits us to access the wisdom and intelligence of the higher chakras.

However it's important to know that even though the "goal" is to have the chakras in alignment, it's not necessarily possible to have them constantly in harmony. You might ask why. Well, much as we'd like it to be, life itself isn't constantly in harmony. There are often moments of flux, change, fear, and discomfort that throw us off-center. Our chakras are constantly moving in and out of alignment, depending on what we are facing. But being aware of the chakra system enables us to direct our energy in a way that will support our return to wellness.

If you are experiencing a blockage in your world, whether emotional, physical, or spiritual, and you take a moment to ask yourself where in your body you are experiencing this discomfort, pain, or uncertainty, you will feel exactly where you are holding it. If you then locate the chakra that either governs that part of the body or surrounds it, you'll have a space you can direct energy to and receive information from in order to center yourself once more. Working with the vibes in this book can help you bring balance to the spaces that need it most.

Kundalini

Kundalini is now the accepted name for what the ancient yogis called the kundalini-Shakti, the "coiled snake of divine feminine energy." It is the primordial creational energy that is held in the base chakra of all human beings.

The idea is that through spiritual practice and devotion, we can encourage this energy to uncoil and move up through the Sushumna channel and all the chakras. When it reaches the brow chakra, the crown chakra opens up and Shakti, femme energy, pierces the heart of the Universe, which is seen as Shiva, masc energy. When they come together, they conjoin as one. This is, however, beyond gender norms and male/female relationships. It is about bringing together the passive and the active and the form and the formless.

When there's that much energy pulsing from the seat of our sensual organs to the crown of our head, it's no wonder it's described as an "ecstatic" or even "orgasmic" experience. It's a mind, body, and spiritual high that no amount of substances can recreate, which is one of the main reasons why kundalini yoga is such an amazing practice for people with a history of addiction or those in recovery.

If you are uncomfortable with the idea of a snake-like energy being within you, please know it's not a literal snake, just a coiled energy form. If this still somewhat frightens you, good! It's when we're feeling fearful that we're on the cusp of a miracle. The fear you are feeling isn't actually the fear of a snake, it's the fear of being powerful, and that's exactly why you're here. Raising your vibration means reclaiming the power of your soul and your capacity to be a light in the world.

How to awaken kundalini

Awakening kundalini is a practice that requires consistency. The ancient yogis prescribed daily *sadhana*, what we call our daily spiritual practice. It's that daily commitment to focusing our energy and remembering we're part of something greater that allows the kundalini to awaken and begin its ascent. So, anything like breathwork, meditation, dance, devotion, prayer, yoga, running, singing, mantras, and chanting will support the awakening of the kundalini.

Essentially, raising your vibration means awakening your kundalini—it's as simple as that.

Overview

I hope that this is helping you understand your spiritual anatomy and what is happening on a subtle level when you are raising your vibration. It might be a lot to take in, but you don't have to remember it all, just be aware that information is available to help you understand what you may be going through. Check back in when you need to.

Here's a breakdown of everything that's been covered so far:

◆ You have a pathway of energy running from the base of your spine to the crown of your head, known as the Sushumna channel.

◆ Femme and masc energies flow through channels known as Ida and Pingala that run alongside this channel, crossing it at seven major points and creating vortices called *chakras*.

◆ Each chakra governs a physical part of the body, including organs and glands that have emotional correlations that can be used as a roadmap to spiritual healing.

◆ By asking our body where an issue or challenge is energetically, we're able to work with the physical parts and the emotional aspects covered by the relevant chakra to promote wellness.

◆ If a chakra lacks energy, by focusing on the areas of our life covered by that chakra, we can bring it back into alignment.

- ◆ When the seven traditional chakras of the body are in alignment, the kundalini energy begins to uncoil and rise through the Sushumna channel, feeding the chakras with life-force.

- ◆ When it has risen through the seven chakras, it creates an ecstatic high called an awakening and we are able to access the "higher" chakras.

- ◆ Access to the higher chakras gives us the wisdom and insight to align with higher purpose and have a greater understanding of our current incarnation.

- ◆ Alignment of all the chakras and awakening of the kundalini help us go beyond wanting to know about God-Source and have a direct experience of creating heaven on Earth.

GOING HIGHER

"Spiritual practice is not just sitting and meditation. Practice is looking, thinking, touching, drinking, eating, and talking. Every act, every breath, and every step can be practice and can help us to become more ourselves."

Thích Nhất Hạnh

You are reading this now because you've made a conscious decision to live a higher-vibrational life. The Universe has heard you and is ready to support you every step of the way.

The key to living a higher-vibrational life is developing a spiritual practice—a toolkit, a routine, a set of practices that you go to every single day to stay conscious and aligned. This book will give you tools, thoughts, and intentions to bring to that practice.

Spiritual practice

Right at the outset it's important to say that your practice is *your* practice. It's all about finding what works for you and fine-tuning it as you progress. Over the years, my own spiritual practice has evolved. Some practices have come and gone and others have stayed with me for 18 years. Some principles, however, remain true for us all.

Make it non-negotiable

What I've noticed is that when the stuff hits the fan, many people let their routine slip, and along with it goes their capacity to stay high-vibrational. It's far better to let your spiritual practice be the anchor that holds you steady in stormy waters.

So, making your spiritual practice non-negotiable is recommended. No matter where you are or what you're doing or what is unfolding in your life, let it be the one constant.

Personally speaking, my practice has been there for me through thick and thin—anxiety, loss, personal health challenges, and family health issues, but also moments of joy. And because I keep it a priority, everyone around me understands and respects it—and benefits from the high vibes that result!

Make it a routine

Routine is linear and spirit is beyond measure, but creating a routine spiritual practice has mega-benefits for both mind and body. Regular meditation practice has been shown to improve sleep and cognitive function, reduce stress, and even thicken the prefrontal cortex, which is the part of the brain that is central to cognitive function, personality expression, and decision-making.

All of that is reason enough to establish a routine, but I also feel that having a routine gives your body, your nervous system, and even your spirit the opportunity to relax and receive love, support, and guidance.

In addition, developing our ability to tune in to the Universe is like strengthening a muscle—it's going to take time, energy, effort, and focus.

So, when should you practice? Morning? Noon? Night? It's totally up to you. It's *your* practice, remember. Personally, though, I think having different things throughout the day is best. That will help you remain centered and balanced. To help you understand how it looks, let me tell you a little bit about my day.

I've never been much of a morning person (and goodness knows, I've tried), so my main practice is an evening one. I usually do a devotional meditation, where I chant a mantra continuously for 11 minutes, and a focused meditation, where I either sit in silence (with background music) or chant some more with Kirtan Kriya (easily found online) from kundalini meditation.

Next, I think about anything I need guidance on, or a particular challenge or issue I'm working through. I'll invite angels to sit with me and will take some time to focus on my blessings and give thanks for my loved ones, security, and wellbeing.

I always close my practice with spiritual protection.

Spiritual protection 101

Spiritual protection is about claiming our space and remembering our wholeness. It's about welcoming divine energy into our energy field so that we don't take on any unwanted energy from other people or environments, or even worldly disasters that we've read about in the paper or seen on the news.

Spiritual protection 101 is when we declare that we aren't going to take on the heaviness of a situation so that we can work with our own incredible light. When we do this, we clear any fear-based shields we have and replace them with ones made of divine love.

There's a difference between spiritual protection and psychic protection: one uses our own energy (psychic) and the other is about allowing our higher power to protect us (spiritual).

Many people have learned how to place a protective light around themselves, but if we don't cleanse our energy and space first, low vibrations may get sealed in that space with us.

Here's a spiritual protection process that will create an armor of light around you. I've based it on a familiar skincare routine. You know the one: the cleanser gets rid of the grime; exfoliating removes anything no longer needed from the surrounding area; the toner firms up the skin; and the moisturizer locks in the goodness.

Administering spiritual protection

Cleanse

First you need to cleanse your energy of any vibes that aren't serving you, perhaps from a challenging conversation, place, or person. There are a couple of ways to do it:

- You can imagine sacred fire energy coming from Mother Earth, burning away any unwanted energy that is attached to you, and transforming it into love.

- You can ask Archangel Michael and his angels to cut any cords of energy that are holding you back by saying a prayer:

"Thank you, Universal Source, Archangel Michael, and angels of protection, for cutting the cords that bind me to people, places, energy, situations, institutions, and any other stuff I no longer need. It feels so good to know you are here. I am safe and free!"

Exfoliate

Exfoliating is all about clearing away any dirt or debris in the surrounding area. In this case, invite Archangel Metatron into your space with the following prayer:

> *"Thank you, Universe, Archangel Metatron, and angels of sacred geometry, for clearing the energetic space that surrounds me. Thank you for removing any lower vibrations, blockages, stagnancies, and anything else that could be standing in the way of love. I welcome your support as you transmute and transform the energy around me. And so it is."*

Tone

Toning is all about firming up the goodness that is already there. When it comes to toning your energy, it's about focusing on an aspect of your present positivity, or harnessing a blessing, or choosing to remember your current state of goodness.

Claim your wholeness by declaring that you are completely in control of your body, because it's the vehicle of your soul. You can say this in your own words, but make sure you are speaking in the present tense and really putting your foot down. Let the Universe and your guides bear witness to the incredible inner strength that you were born with. My favorite declaration is powerful, simple, and effective:

> *"I am the keeper of my mind and body. Wherever love is present, fear is a stranger. Love is here!"*

When I say, "Love is here," I tap my heart three times, so I can feel physically what I know deep within.

Moisturize

When you are moisturizing your energy, you are essentially putting on a coating to lock in the goodness. This is the step that everyone knows from books and healing modality trainings, but it won't be truly effective unless the previous steps have been taken.

The key is to ensure the protection you are welcoming in is from Source, rather than a projection of your own energy.

◆ Visualize a piercing light of whatever color you are drawn to coming from the heart of Source and washing through your entire body and energy.

◆ Then say this prayer:

> *"Thank you, Source light, for shining upon me, around me, and through every aspect of my life. I am protected by your light. I am safe in your light. And so it is."*

As you say this, visualize angels standing around you. Source light is always drawn to them and they will be holding you in a space of safety.

My daily practice

That's my main practice. But there are other elements that I weave into my day:

◆ I start with prayer and gratitude, inviting the Universe to lead the way through my day.

◆ I bless my food.

- ◆ I pick angel/oracle cards for inspiration and guidance.

- ◆ I check in with the season and the moon.

- ◆ I watch a TED talk on YouTube or listen to an interesting podcast for inspiration.

- ◆ Anytime something wonderful happens, I exclaim, "Thank you, Universe!" and sometimes, *"Wahe guru"* (Wonderful teacher within).

- ◆ Throughout the day I say affirmations inspired by the work of Louise Hay.

- ◆ When I'm having conversations, I share what I am grateful for in others to inspire uplifting energy.

- ◆ I steer away from arguments, moaning, or complaining, if possible.

- ◆ I do yoga often and some other form of movement at least once a day.

And that's how it looks for me.

Over time you'll fine-tune your own daily practice, but I'd recommend checking in with your vibration throughout the day and doing the inner work to raise it.

Here are some ways to do that.

Meditation

Meditation is the foundation of any spiritual practice. For me, meditation isn't about switching the mind off, it's about switching the mind on. That's why people speak about mindfulness—the mind is full.

The key to meditation is learning how to sit and be at peace with yourself. I recommend starting slowly. That might be sitting with your eyes closed, focusing on your breath, and listening to a relaxing piece of music for around five minutes daily. Extend it as you wish.

Breathwork

Prana is the Sanskrit word for "life-force" and in yoga, there is no difference between life and breath. Breathwork is powerful because it revitalizes your body and allows you to have a visceral body–mind connection with life. Trying different breathing techniques (*pranayama*) is highly recommended.

Mantras

Mantra meditation is when you repeat a word, sentence, or affirmation over and over again in order to enter a transcendental/meditative state. Research has shown that practicing this daily can significantly lower your blood pressure, improve blood glucose and insulin levels, and promote better functioning of the nervous system.

What's powerful about mantra meditation is that being so focused on the rhythm of the mantra and your breath, you can't think about anything else, and thus it provides an opportunity to escape your own head.

Exercise/yoga

I recommend having a way of uniting breath, mind, and body, for when you are in touch with your body, you are holding space for your soul to reveal itself. Exercise and yoga are both wonderful for connecting with your body and mind, and can have positive effects on your physical health as well.

Weaving a run into your week or participating in some form of yoga, even if it's chair yoga, is a great way to begin aligning all of your energy centers with your breath and creating a sense of openness and spiritual connection.

Self-care

Acts of self-care help you develop self-respect, boundaries, and ultimately self-love. Self-care looks different to everyone, but it can be simply taking the time to have a sea-salt bath, go to a meditation class, or even put on soothing moisturizer before going to bed. Remember your body is the home of your soul, and everything you do for your body, you do for your soul. Also, acts of self-care have been known to promote better sleep, reduce stress, improve focus, and strengthen relationships!

High-vibe attraction

"As you think, you vibrate. As you vibrate, you attract."

ABRAHAM–HICKS

When you develop a daily spiritual practice, you reconfigure your vibration, creating a golden aura that draws golden experiences to you. This is the Law of Attraction in operation.

The Law of Attraction

The Law of Attraction is one of the most popular spiritual teachings of the 21st century. It's quite simple: like attracts like, energy attracts energy, thoughts attract experiences.

This means we have a huge input into what unfolds in our world.

Now, there's a good chance you're thinking, *Well, why do bad things happen to good people?* Truth be told, I don't know the reasons behind every challenge in a good person's life. And it's important to remember that the human experience can be challenging, heavy, and unpredictable.

If something challenging has happened in your life, you might also be thinking, *If my thoughts create my life, what thinking made that happen?*, but it's important not to try and figure out why a certain event has happened, but to realize that within you there is infinite potential that can contribute to change, healing, and even miracles.

The Law of Attraction can help you refine your energy, so that you can attract loving and positive experiences, and should anything go wrong, you have a tool to support your recovery.

Every one of your thoughts, feelings, actions, non-actions, ideas, beliefs, emotions, and feelings is contributing to the unfoldment of your life. But—and this is a public service announcement—don't start to get worried about every negative thought. You are a spiritual being having a human experience, and being human isn't always easy. It's okay to have off-days, worries, and concerns. In fact, that's why you develop a spiritual practice!

When you develop this practice, all of the inner work you're doing raises your vibration, and your good intentions will begin to outweigh the beliefs and narratives that are no longer serving you.

That's why many people who are living a spiritual life are faced with challenges or have dark nights of the ego, for they're detoxing from all their old ideas, beliefs, and stories, and it can take a lot of energy and focus to let go of them for good.

That's why I'm here to share with you the ultimate tool for raising your vibration.

It's feelings.

When I first learned about the Law of Attraction, I wanted to manifest anything and everything I could—a new car, money in the bank, a leaner body... I'd write down lists, visualize the material items in my life, and speak them into creation. It worked. But when my twenties were coming to an end, I realized that the *things* weren't what I was looking for...

I wanted a new car because I wanted to feel good enough and be seen.

I wanted money in the bank because I wanted to feel safe and secure.

I wanted to lose weight because I wanted to feel more lovable.

> **One day it just clicked: I wasn't looking for the
> things, I was looking for the feelings behind them.**

So I began to shift my energy, and instead of writing down lists of *things*, I made *feelings* my goals. Not only that, I turned my focus in my spiritual practice over to gratitude, service, and devotion. Instead of constantly asking for more, I expressed genuine gratitude for all I had.

I wasn't prepared for what happened from that moment on: everything I could have ever wanted and more was delivered into my life.

That was the high-vibrational Law of Attraction at work.

So, ask yourself:

◆ What is it I dream of?

◆ What is it I really want?

◆ How do I think this will make me feel?

When you get to the bottom of it, instead of asking for the thing, work on feeling the way you want to feel. When you align your energy with that feeling, there's a good chance you'll manifest that dream, or, even better, you'll get the upgraded version.

High-vibe energies

There are three energies that I recommend embodying in order to attract blessings, abundance, and a high-vibe life.

Gratitude

Gratitude is one of the highest vibrations we can have. It has been known to improve our overall state of happiness, improve sleep, and create hope for the future.

You can feel grateful for your loved ones, for nature, or even for life itself. As soon as you bring your awareness to what you are grateful for, you begin to create an energy that will attract more reasons to be grateful.

Devotion

Devotion is defined as love, loyalty, and worship. It's when you bring your awareness, focus, and energy to someone or something you have a deep unconditional love and respect for. When you devote your energy to something without expectation, you generate a bright light that draws in experiences and energies that reflect your devotion.

In the *Bhagavad Gita*, Krishna, an incarnation of the divine, says:

> *"When a person is devoted to something with complete faith, I unify their faith in that. Then, when their faith is completely unified, they shall gain the object of their devotion."*

Therefore, when you devote yourself to your family, your children, your spiritual practice, the Universe will replenish your being with the feeling that you are also cherished, loved, and accepted in the same way.

Kindness

If something is good for you physiologically, I can guarantee that it will be good for your vibration. And kindness can shift your energy, lift your mood, and improve your physical health all at once.

So, if you're feeling the need to boost your vibration, focus on performing acts of service and kindness. When you are genuinely kind to others, the Universe will be kind to you in return.

High-vibe opportunities

When you begin to consciously raise your vibration, you shift your point of attraction, as we have seen. What does this mean for you?

Raising your vibration creates a magnetic aura around you, and if you ever played with a magnet as a child, you'll know that all magnets have polarity: one side repels, the other side attracts. On a vibrational level, this means that energies that are no longer in alignment with your energy field will be pushed away. That can be challenging for personal relationships and other prominent lifestyle choices. But there is method in the moments that feel like madness. They aren't tests, they're opportunities.

In my early teens, for example, when I was absolutely obsessed with studying spirituality, it put pressure on my friendships and for a long time it made me feel like an outsider, but somewhere along the way everything clicked into place. I realized that studying spirituality was a personal choice and if I kept throwing that stuff down the throats of people who hadn't made that choice, it would only push them away from me. I had to respect everyone else's life choices if I wanted them to respect mine.

To this day I am still friends with the vast majority of my friends from high school and my main group of friends is still the same. Though supportive of my career and lifestyle, they don't take any interest in my spiritual work, and that's okay with me. Even my atheist friends send me screen shots of their iPhones when they see 11:11, though... Yes, the Universe could be recruiting them!

When you begin to raise your vibration, you are given the opportunity to see that every relationship is an assignment and to see the divine in all beings, whatever their lifestyle choices. Our role when we raise our vibration is to move beyond the boundaries of human relationships and embody a love that is unconditional. Unconditional love has no space for judgment—it respects everyone for who they are.

Having said this, if there are changes happening around you that feel beyond your control, here's an important message:

> *The Universe may be removing from your life the people and energies that are not supporting the vibe you are creating.*

This doesn't mean that the folks or life experiences that are moving away are less spiritual than you or on a lower vibration, it's just that they're no longer on the same vibration.

Rest assured that new experiences and connections will come to you in one way or another. You might find that when you begin to raise your vibration, your community shows up in the form of friendships opening up all around the world. This doesn't mean you're pushing people away, it's more that you all have your own personal missions but can still lean on one another for support.

Just recently I was speaking to a dear friend on the phone about how far apart we lived and she said, "Do you think it's because we're placed where we need to be?"

My instant answer was: "*Yes!*"

> *Where you are is where you are needed.*
>
> *Where you are is where there are opportunities to heal.*
>
> *Raise your vibration where you are.*

You may want to align absolutely every single part of your life with spirituality by quitting your job and cutting off your friends group, but this isn't what you need. Wanting to leave your old life behind is ultimately spiritual bypassing.

Spiritual bypassing

You may never have heard of spiritual bypassing, but there's a good chance you've encountered it on your journey. It's using spiritual terminology to avoid dealing with something that requires your attention. Ultimately, it's avoiding the assignments that have been given to you.

It's important to flag here that all of us within the spiritual community are guilty of spiritual bypassing, and sometimes we're not aware of it. But it's also important to acknowledge that it can be harmful to individuals and even communities. We are here to be fully human, but it's essential that we're mindful of others and aware of everything that's going on around us, so that we can make a loving and compassionate contribution.

At the time of writing, for example, we're emerging from the Covid-19 pandemic. During the initial outbreak, I held back from speaking about it and simply commented that whatever was going on, many people's lives were being affected, and it was important to remember that. Some spiritual teachers and practitioners, however, said that only those with a low vibration would be affected by the highly contagious virus. This is spiritual bypassing. When people believe they are "beyond" a worldwide issue like a pandemic, or that they are untouchable because they have a high-vibe lifestyle, things become problematic.

Another example would be participating in a spiritual practice from another culture, even though you have received feedback that it's offensive to people from that culture. For example, a white person with no Indigenous connection might wear an Indigenous headdress and say, "Oh, my spirit guides are Indigenous peoples," or "I was an Indigenous person in a past life." That could be true, but it wouldn't give them the right to participate in offensive behavior.

Raising our vibration doesn't mean we get a pass on harmful behavior. Ever. In fact, we're held even more accountable (rightly so), since we're spending so much time on becoming aware.

"That's not very spiritual"

You know when you see a "spiritual" person acting in a way that isn't in alignment with what you feel is spiritual? When you find out that your favorite meditation teacher isn't vegan, for example, or that they drink alcohol? "That's not very spiritual of you" is a comment that might well come to mind.

This is a limiting way of thinking, though. Ultimately, it's the New Age version of the "holier than thou" mindset that was pushed heavily by Fundamentalism.

Don't be concerned about how someone else is navigating their spirituality; be concerned about your own karma.

> *Being spiritual is about living a life of authenticity,*
> *while recognizing you are part of something greater.*

Anxiety, depression, and mental health

I think a lot of us who are seeking a higher-vibe life are likely to have encountered anxiety, depression, or other mental health issues along the way. So, it's important to know that you can still have a high vibration when you are dealing with challenges to your mental and emotional wellbeing. You may have seen images of "perfect" people practicing yoga or meditation, but let me tell you straight, in order to heal sometimes you have to witness your challenges, feel the darkest of emotions, or even push through trauma. And I can tell you from experience that having a spiritual practice and a high-vibe life doesn't mean you'll never have anxiety or depression.

I've recently had to navigate overwhelming anxiety myself. I hadn't had panic attacks since I was a teenager, but after having Covid-19, I ended up getting recurring heart palpitations that culminated in full-blown episodes of anxiety that I couldn't explain. It led me into such a dark spiral of uncertainty that I found myself having nightmare thoughts that were genuinely terrifying.

During that time, lots of other people and even family members would say, "You're supposed to be the high-vibe guy!" as if that meant I was supposed to completely transcend being human and navigating human emotions.

We're all human. But remember:

> *You can raise your vibration while navigating mental health challenges.*

> *Your anxiety isn't manifesting negative things in your life.*

Your spiritual practice will far outweigh any anxiety or depression. Having a space where you can go to focus on what will make you feel good, or at least better, will attract positivity, blessings, and healing opportunities to you.

If I'm feeling anxious, I'll anchor into my spiritual practice, even if it's a challenge to do so. Fortunately, I know that what's important isn't how deep the practice is, it's the fact that I've shown up for it.

You can't high-vibe your way out of being human

Another thing is the human thing. There's a lot of information out there right now regarding the shifting of dimensions. People will often talk about moving into the fifth dimension and present the idea that when you're high-vibrational, you're almost superhuman.

Now there's no doubt that our mind can affect our life and even heal our body (or at least contribute), but that doesn't mean that we become invincible. We signed up to have a human experience, and living a high-vibrational life can result in a *better* human experience, but it doesn't mean we can transcend being human entirely.

Some of the highest-vibrational people I know—and because of the industry I'm in, I've had the absolute honor and pleasure of connecting with some of the world's leading doctors, scientists, motivators, and healers—still get sick, face challenges, and have aspects of their life that require healing.

Being high-vibe doesn't mean you'll avoid challenges, but it does mean you'll have more chance of surmounting them, because you're doing the inner work that will lead to freedom.

So, let's look at that inner work more closely.

Tuning in

"You are the soul of the Universe
and your name is love."

RUMI

The key to developing your spiritual connection is encouraging your human shell to settle so that the spirit within can rise up. It's called tuning in.

You can do it anywhere. I remember being in India studying Ashtanga yoga and finding tears of devotion pouring down my pink cheeks when we tuned in early one morning. I had arrived. I was home. But not in India—I was home *in myself*.

That's what the practice of tuning in is all about. It's about calling your energy home and calling up your soul self, the great teacher within—the voice of resilience, spirit, and strength that will support you in creating heaven on Earth.

Then you can set a clear intention to raise your vibration and make a deep connection with Source.

Do this before you do any of the exercises in this book, or any spiritual practice, such as picking angel cards, working with crystals, or even meditating. You'll find that everything that follows will be clearer.

Here's my step-by-step guide:

- Take a moment to shake off the day. Stand up if you can and just shake it all out.

- Sit down. On the floor, in a chair—wherever is comfy.

- Take several deep breaths.

- Bring your hands into the prayer position and begin to rub your palms together. This activates your energy. When your hands are hot, hold them in prayer.

- Set an intention to call up your inner teacher. You may even say this prayer:

> *"Great teacher within, thank you for standing at the forefront of my heart and mind, reminding me that I am one with the Source of creation. Thank you for leading the way in my spiritual practice and my life."*

- Take a moment to imagine or feel the great teacher rising up.

- Dedicate the merit of your practice as follows:

> *"I set the clear intention that this practice today is dedicated to the greatest good of all beings. Whatever is gained from this practice, may it be dedicated to the liberation and healing of all beings in all four corners of this world. I set the intention that this practice creates a light that reaches out to the children and the animals of this world, who sometimes do not have a voice. May this light lift them—to be seen, to be heard, and to be helped.*
>
> *I say this for the highest good of all.*
>
> *And so it is."*

- You are now officially tuned in.

How to use this book

Now you're ready, what next?

The next part of this book offers 77 "vibes"—spiritual lessons and techniques to raise your vibration. All of them are easy and accessible. All of them can be done anywhere, anytime, even in public!

There are seven vibes for the kundalini and each of the traditional chakras. In numerology, seven is the number of divine magic and manifestation.

Then there are five vibes for each of the four "higher" chakras. These are said to exist in the fifth dimension and I wanted to honor uniting with that.

Finally, there is a lesson to create a magnetic aura, followed by a closing activation to embody your light.

The intention is that the opening vibes awaken the kundalini and the sections that follow trace its ascent though the chakra system to a higher vibration.

How many of these lessons you do is totally up to you. You can work your way through them all in one sitting, or you can do a section as a set, or you can do one or two a day, or one every now and then. Whatever you are drawn to is absolutely right for you.

You can also trust the Universe. Say a prayer along the lines of:

"Thank you, Universe, for guiding me to a lesson that will best support my current situation."

Then take that section of the book and open it at a "random" page. That page will be synchronistically aligned to what you need to work on to raise your vibration.

Whatever way you use this book, know that it will always be guided, because the Universe is in every moment.

Awaken
(Kundalini)

At the base of our spine, in the core of our being, is the spark of creation, the pure divine life-force that connects us to the infinity of life itself: our kundalini-Shakti. It is visualized as a divine serpent that uncoils and moves upward through our subtle body, replenishing us and helping us fulfill our purpose.

Its "Shakti" aspect is an indication that it is feminine in nature— cyclic, beyond the constrictions of linear thinking—and thus encouraging us to surrender and trust in the spiritual process.

When it awakens, we begin to make more conscious choices and live in a more heart-centered way. We may even find that we unlock the wisdom or clarity required to overcome previous challenges.

I believe that awareness and clarity are by-products of the inner work. We cannot know exactly what to expect in life, because all of us are different, with different ways of being and seeing, and different gifts to offer. But I believe that through awakening our kundalini, we will find the keys to creating a more loving and conscious experience on Earth.

The time and energy we spend in meditation, spiritual study, and consistent remembrance that we are spirit embodied provide the perfect space for the kundalini to rise. The goal is to let this energy reach the crown chakra. When it does so, we are able to have a direct experience of the divine, merging the higher dimensions with the physical world.

VIBE 1
Answering the call

You have been called here. By the power that created you and the power that is within you.

Before you were in this life and this body, you danced among the stars. Your human shell is made up of the particles of former stars. You have the Universe within.

But there's a good chance that somewhere along the way, you've forgotten your divine origin. There's also a good chance that the Universe has sent you a number of wake-up calls—moments that have helped you realize that you are more than just a mortal shell; moments that have reminded you of the power of love and of the Universe; moments that have guided you to realize that there has to be something more than just existing; moments when you've felt called to live in more conscious and high-vibrational way.

These wake-up calls have come to remind
you that you are never alone.

Angels, ancestors, and spiritual guides are with you.

They are with you now, lighting your
way to a higher vibration.

Through "activation." An activation is an intention to awaken an aspect of your spiritual power that has been asleep. It's giving yourself permission to live in a way that leads you to fulfill your highest potential. It's stopping fighting the hesitations your ego has been forcing upon you, making you question if you're going crazy or not, and saying, "Yes!" to something greater.

It's allowing your kundalini to awaken.

That time is now.

VIBE OF THE DAY

"Dear Universe,

I have heard your call.

Thank you for sending me reminders to help me realize that there is more to life than the way I have been living. I realize that the challenges that I have faced have been windows of opportunity and today I say, 'Yes!'

I say, 'Yes!' to living with more purpose.

I say, 'Yes!' to experiencing more support and enrichment.

I say, 'Yes!' to manifesting a life I love.

I choose to activate the divine force within me, the pure primal life-force. Thank you, divine life-force, for pulsing through my entire being.

I awaken to my truest self.

And so it is."

VIBE 2
Tapping into the Universe

There's a huge difference between spirituality and religion.

♦ Religion is a set of man-made rules and dogmas about God-Source.

♦ Spirituality is a set of practices aimed at facilitating the *direct experience* of God-Source.

You are here because you know that it is your divine right to have a personal experience of Source. You are deserving of having a direct experience of the Universe because you *are* the Universe. The place you have come from is also a place you have never left. Your soul is multi-dimensional and there's an aspect of it still in the heart of the Universe.

So, when you do the deep dive to knowing yourself on a deeper level, you also initiate the experience of knowing your Creator, of knowing the all-encompassing Universe.

Quite simply, when you tap into the Universe, you also tap into yourself; when you tap into yourself, you also tap into the Universe. You are one and the same.

The great inner teacher is the part of you that knows it has never left the heart of it all—when you listen to it, you know that too.

You are part of it all.

When you begin to raise your vibration, you begin to create the lived experience of heaven on Earth, where you transcend the man-made stories about "God" and experience a presence that is all-encompassing, unconditional love.

Simply being willing to experience it gives permission for the ancient wisdom that you have gathered throughout your lifetimes to awaken.

VIBE OF THE DAY

"To know the Universe is to know myself.

To know myself is to know the Universe.

I tap into the ancient life-force within, giving permission for wisdom to rise up.

I am willing to have a direct experience of Source.

Moving beyond the contradictions and restrictions of ego and fear, I reach into the heart of creation and find the pieces of myself that are ready to be known.

I am one with all that is."

VIBE 3
Breath is life-force

Breathing is so important. The ancient yogis called breath *prana*, which is the Sanskrit word for "life-force." So, when we are breathing deeply, we are drawing divine light energy into our body.

Quite simply, our breath regenerates our body. It brings oxygen to our cells. It keeps us alive.

Our lung capacity is actually quite large, but we generally don't use all of it. Most people under pressure only breathe using the top part of their lungs, which means that the top of the chest and the throat area are receiving the energy, but it's not extending much further than that.

When too much energy builds up in one place like this, we add to our stress rather than relieve it. So, instead, draw deeply on that nourishing life-force.

VIBE OF THE DAY

Today you are encouraged to breathe using the full capacity of your lungs and draw pure life-force into the whole of your being.

Let this simple breathing technique be something you come back to time and time again:

- Bring your hands to your abdomen. Place them on either side of your belly and breathe into them. Feel the natural rhythm of your breath flowing in and out of your body. Do this for 8–10 breaths.

- Bring your hands to your sides. Wrap them around your ribcage and breathe into them. Feel your diaphragm expanding with every in-breath. Do this for 8–10 breaths.

- Place your fingers on your collarbone. Allow your hands to rest gently on your chest and breathe into them. Feel your chest lifting and your throat filling with *prana* with every in-breath. Do this for 8–10 breaths.

- When you have finished this sequence of breaths, you may want to do it without your hands simply by breathing into all these spaces. Linking the breath in the belly, middle body, and upper body forms the full yogic breath that connects body, mind, and soul.

"When I breathe, I unite with the power that created me.
When I breathe, I am reminded that I am not alone.
When I breathe, I restore my being with pure life-force."

VIBE 4
You are not alone

Everything in the Universe is energy, including you. For that reason, you don't walk this path alone. You are connected to everyone and everything that is, was, and ever will be.

The moment you are born you are given the gift of free will. This starts to unfold as you develop, and when you enter adult life, you get to decide what you want to do, when, where, and with whom.

The Universe would love to help you—it would love to help us all, but it can't do so unless we choose to ask.

Independence is seen as strength on Earth. Being able to do your own thing and not ask for help seems to be positive. The downside is that many people feel it is "weak" to ask for help. In spirituality we honor independence, but we also note that there is another option: co-creation.

In order to raise your vibration and move beyond the limited thoughts that can make you feel isolated and unsupported, you have to surrender the idea of being independent and move into the space of co-creating with the Creator. (Your vision of the Creator will be different from mine, and it can be "God" or it can just be "life," but whatever works for you is right.)

Today, realize that you don't have to do everything on your own. You are walking this path with your Creator and with the energy you are co-creating. When you realize this, a huge weight will be lifted from your shoulders. Essentially you will be allowing the weight of your own world to be held by a power that is greater than you are.

VIBE OF THE DAY

Today's vibe is all about setting an intention. There's no right or wrong way to do it. Maybe meditate on it, say it, pray it, or dance it. If the intention is right, the vibe is right!

"Today I choose to surrender my independence.

I choose to remember that I don't walk this path alone.

I am co-creating my world with my Creator.

Angels dance around me.

As everything in the Universe is made of energy, including me, I choose to welcome the energy of support and love into my life.

Today I choose to walk with the Universe, knowing it's supporting me all the way."

VIBE 5
The present is a gift

There is no place more powerful than the present. But most of us choose to think about the past instead, or what we need to do next.

When we begin raising our vibration, though, the Universe will call us back to the present so that we can understand its true power. It's through our personal experience of the present that our gifts are revealed.

Remember that when you welcome miracles and gifts into your life, you don't deprive others of them. In fact, by recognizing the beauty of the Universe, accepting its support, and feeling grateful for it, you are demonstrating to others how they can feel supported too.

Today, up your vibes by recognizing that raising your vibration is not only a gift you give to yourself, but a gift you offer to others simply through your smile.

When you arrive in the present moment, people don't just see you, they feel they know you, for when you come home to yourself, you allow the light of your soul to be seen and the ancient spiritual energy within you to awaken.

VIBE OF THE DAY

Today's technique is all about getting back to the present.

Imagine for a moment that there's a beautiful golden light above your head. That golden light is moving through every cell of your skin. It is moving through your vital organs and through the air you are breathing. It is replenishing your lungs and dancing through the flow of your blood. It's moving to the tips of your fingers and toes.

The light that you are imagining is life itself, and essentially it's made of love. It's moving through us all, but because we are so busy with what's going on in our lives we forget about this beautiful connection to the Universe.

When you choose to remember this light and to breathe with ease, knowing you are part of it, you recognize the gift of life. And when you recognize the gift of life, you raise your vibration so high that you ignite a light in other people.

"I choose to breathe with ease, knowing
that life is present with me now.

Knowing I am connected to life makes me feel safe and alive.

I offer this present to others through my smile today.

I smile, knowing that life is smiling upon and through me.

My presence is a gift."

VIBE 6

What you are seeking, you were born to create

Your life hasn't happened by accident. It isn't a mistake. You chose to come here, into this life and this body, for every incarnation is an opportunity to teach and to learn.

Not everything was set out for you on your journey—you have always had a choice—and every lesson and challenge has been an unraveling of previous steps, like a labyrinth unwinding, revealing only what is required to bring you closer to yourself.

In moments of fear and restriction, you may have been led further from who you are today, but often in order to find something, it first has to be lost.

In every challenge you have faced, you have been presented with an opportunity. It may not always have been easy to see that, but there has always been something to learn. Something that can help heal the hearts of others.

Every step you have taken has brought you to this space—a space where you are realizing you are more than you thought you were. Much more.

> **You exist within the Universe, but the Universe also exists within you.**

This reminds you that your life has meaning, and you are now arriving in a space where you can live with meaning.

What you are seeking, you were born to create.

Lessons and challenges are opportunities to teach.

Your story has power that can heal.

All your thoughts, steps, and energies have brought you this opportunity to serve, be served, and live with purpose.

It is not your duty to know every step of the way, but your acceptance of this life mission will present you with gateways of opportunity to make this planet a better space than it was when you came to it.

VIBE OF THE DAY

"In every challenge I have faced, there has been a lesson.

The lessons I have learned are information to share.

When I share, I teach. When I teach, I learn.

*Through sharing my learning, I am led
closer to living my purpose.*

*For what I have been seeking
is what I was born to create."*

VIBE 7

*I am my body, but I am also much more
(kundalini activation)*

Your body is a moving miracle. It's the vehicle that holds all of the vital organs that keep you alive and well, but also the shell that holds your mind and soul.

Through your body you are able to access the intelligence held within your brain and experience the divine intelligence of the Universe.

You are remembering that even though you have this physical shell that needs to be loved and cared for, you are so much more. You are remembering that you are the Universe.

Through this remembering, you can awaken and activate the kundalini, the divine spark within.

Through this awakening, you give permission for the soul aspect of your being to be revealed through your life.

That is seriously miraculous stuff.

At first it can be hard to comprehend, but on some level you know that it is your truth, for you wouldn't be here doing this work if you didn't believe it was possible.

So, what *is* possible? When you remember who you are, you begin to see the interconnectedness of all things and beings and realize that there is significance in what can feel like your insignificance.

You are part of the bigger picture and you are here to contribute to the bigger picture through your body and through remembering you are more just than a body.

If you haven't fully grasped this, just be willing to experience it, and your kundalini will take care of the rest. Through the lessons that follow this activation, you will begin to open your spiritual eyes and see that you are more than you thought and that there is more to the world than you ever realized.

VIBE OF THE DAY

"I am my body, but I am more than my body.

I am my soul, but I am more than my soul.

I am willing to see the connectedness of all things.

I am body, but I am soul.

I am soul, but I am body.

I am willing to experience this reality as my reality.

Kundalini, rise, ignite my inner vision. I am ready to see from my soul through my body.

And so it is."

Ground
(Base chakra)

The base chakra, also known as the root chakra, is found between the tip of the tailbone and the lower back. In Sanskrit it is known as Muladhara, "Root Support," and it is the chakra that governs the lower half of the body, including the feet, the legs, and the base and lower discs of the spine. Ruled by the element of Earth, on an emotional level it governs our sense of safety, security, home, and family. It represents our "backbone," our way of asserting our right to be on planet Earth. Traditionally, it is said to be red when it's in balance.

When our base chakra is in alignment, we'll feel safe, strong, and rooted in our day-to-day life. Even if we're experiencing uncertainty or challenges, our backbone will be strong and we'll trust that we'll get to where we need to be.

If there's a lack of energy in this center, there's a good chance that on an emotional level there will either be a deep-rooted fear that we're not safe or a feeling that we don't deserve to be here ("here" being "on the Earth," but it can extend to our personal and professional life).

If you were building a house on unsteady ground, the house would also be unsteady. On an energetic level, this is the chakra that provides the firm foundation that allows our vibration to rise up.

If you want to bring strength and balance to this space, you need to look at the aspects of your life that govern your sense of safety and security. All of the lessons in this section are dedicated to this.

VIBE 8
You are safe

You have answered the call to leave this Earth in a better state than when you came to it. That's ultimately what raising your vibration is all about.

What does this have to do with feeling safe? If you are feeling unsafe in yourself, your world can reflect this. You may find yourself in circumstances or situations that echo this feeling. This can be extremely difficult to shake, especially if you have been subjected to a difficult start in life or a lifestyle that has chipped away at your self-worth.

But you have been called here and today's message from the Universe is simple and clear:

You deserve to feel safe.

All that you do for yourself is what you offer up to the world. Therefore, feeling safe and experiencing safety is a purposeful mission. Feeling safe creates a wave of healing and change that washes over your world, and bit by bit this can contribute to greater healing.

In order to move to a safe place, you have to acknowledge all the fears that you have. Taking time to "feel them out" allows you to recognize that feelings are just feelings and they don't have to be your truth. You can change the narrative.

This isn't about avoidance. This is about recognition. Feel how you need to feel before working on how you want to feel.

The way to overcome your fears is to remember that even though you can be hurt emotionally or physically, *the real you* can never be tarnished.

> **Your soul is eternal and unbreakable. Let that be the light that guides you to safety.**

VIBE OF THE DAY

"There is no place safer for me than my body.

My body is the home of my soul.

My outer self is a reflection of my inner self.

My soul is the true and real aspect of myself and it can never be broken, tarnished, or damaged.

My soul is healed and whole.

Today I claim my safety, because the light of my soul shines within a light of protection.

I am safe!"

VIBE 9

Give thanks to the Earth

The Earth is a wonderful place to be. Every day this incredible planet holds us, hosts us, and nourishes us. Shelter, food, and water all come from "her." She's so loving and giving.

Yet so many people walking the Earth take her for granted. They take, take, take, and never spend a moment feeling grateful for all the incredible things she offers us. When they see natural disasters, some people get the idea that Mother Earth is punishing us for mistreating her, but that's not the case. She's simply self-correcting. These moments are "wake-up calls" offering opportunities for healing and change.

Mother Earth is like any loving and giving mother—she will do anything she can for her children and will continue to do so with all of her might. The huge problem is that, like most mothers, she will put her children first, giving all of her resources until she has no more.

The message from the Universe is clear:

"Protect Mother Earth."

When you begin to raise your vibration, you will naturally want to support the planet. The more spiritually aware you become, the more conscious of the Earth you become, and the more you feel called to look after her.

You can begin with small shifts—something as simple as picking up litter from the beach, forest, park, or street, or feeding the birds, planting wildflowers to help the bees, or supporting a charity planting trees. Maybe you are already doing this. Ask yourself what more you can do.

Helping Mother Earth feels good, and if it feels good, it means you are on purpose and raising your vibration. What's more:

When you raise your energy, you raise that of the planet as well.

VIBE OF THE DAY

"Mother Earth,

I am your child. Thank you for being here for me. It feels so good to be here with you.

I thank you for holding me, hosting me, and nourishing me. I am so grateful.

Today I vow to do my very best to help you in your evolution. I know that as you grow and evolve, I will too.

Thank you for all of the blessings you have given me. I feel very blessed."

VIBE 10

Abundance is a state of mind

The Universe is abundant in energy—it has no beginning and no end. You are a spark from the heart of the Universe, so you are naturally abundant too.

Within modern spirituality, "abundance" is a word that is energetically aligned with riches, but riches don't always have to be how much you have in the bank or how many other physical blessings you have.

On Earth, we have a tendency to measure how rich we are by the things we have and the achievements of our life. But when we do this, we have a tendency to measure or even limit our worth, and this brings the danger that we will never feel good enough.

Know that the Universe isn't measuring your worth, for you are a part of it and therefore perfect in every facet of your being. And as the Universe itself is abundant in nature, abundance is what it believes you deserve.

Everything you "have" on this Earth is just an external representation of how rich you feel within, and you can never be rich if you feel poor. Reclaim this story. Rewrite the narrative. You are richer than you think:

- ◆ You are rich in opportunity.
- ◆ You are rich in curiosity.
- ◆ You are rich in experience.
- ◆ You are rich in choice.

Shifting your perspective on how abundant you actually are, internally and spiritually, can support the creation and experience of physical riches in your life too.

VIBE OF THE DAY

Abundance is a state of mind. Today, tune in to the blessings you have. Tune in to the love of your people, your gifts, and the blessings of your world. Make it your practice to notice your riches.

"Today I recognize that my life is full of abundance and fulfillment in so many ways.

I am rich because I am a soul filled with divine light.

I allow this light to shine through my day and my entire life.

It feels so good to be this blessed.

I am rich in mind, body, and spirit.

I am destined to experience abundance.

Thank you, Universe. I recognize that abundance is a state of mind."

VIBE 11

Kindness is cool

The spiritual Law of Attraction is simple. It teaches that whatever we believe to be true is what we're going to experience in the world. It's really important to bring this ancient sacred teaching into your awareness so that you can cultivate a mindset that is working *for* you, not against you.

Your inner dialogue has a lot to do with how you experience the world. Are the conversations in your mind mostly loving? Or are there loads of fears floating around?

It's okay to have fears floating around, but it's important to know that your natural state—the greatest part of you—is love.

In honoring that natural loving state, you are encouraged to have kind conversations with yourself. Go to your mirror today and find out what starts to happen there. Do you start criticizing what you see and who you are? How can you change your inner conversation to be more loving? How can you be kinder to yourself?

As you already know, your body is the home of your soul. It's the temple that is holding your divine light, so why not honor that and speak to yourself in a kind way?

If you begin to speak lovingly to yourself, but find that your ego self, that inner critic, puts up a fight, be kind to them too. Say, "Thanks for sharing, but today I choose kindness."

When you are kind to yourself, it allows your energy to be open to kindness on all levels. You give those you love an easier time, and they give you an easier time too. Your kindness to yourself is a gift of kindness to the world. And you're setting an example for those around you and the generations that will follow.

VIBE OF THE DAY

"Today I choose to be kind to myself.

Today I choose to honor my soul.

Today I recognize that my natural state is good.

I allow all false thoughts and criticisms to fade away.

My kindness is a prayer to the divine
within and the divine in others.

I allow kindness to flow through all areas in my life."

VIBE 12
The Universe has a better plan

Sometimes it can be very easy to be pulled into the mindset that life is working against you, but it's not! The Universe is always working with your intentions so that you experience what is for your highest good, rather than what you think you want.

The Universe wants you to be happy, abundant, and fulfilled.

It loves you more than words can describe.

Let it support you.

Trusting that the Universe is always working for your highest good is essential if you want to raise your vibration.

There will be times when you get carried away with a situation or when fear gets in the way, but know that any passionate emotions that arise inside you are okay and a reminder that you care deeply about whatever situation you are in. Having emotionally overwhelming moments doesn't tamper with your overall vibration, so don't let a challenging moment stand between you and the peace you deserve.

If you feel that having a tantrum or a meltdown is the only way to bust through the blocks or express the emotions you are feeling, find a place where you can have some privacy, then let it all out. When you have an emotional clear-out, you create more space in which to regain your composure and experience the support the Universe can offer you.

If you are in a situation that feels stagnant or is going "wrong," don't let your ego or fears make you think your prayers aren't being answered or your manifestations aren't unfolding. Know that when you put your energy out there, the Universe responds. If you put it out there and then snap into impatience, though, you're going to be made to wait. This is where change is required.

The Universe always has a better plan.
Be open to that better plan.

Be open to shifting your perception.

That's how you raise your vibration.

VIBE OF THE DAY

Today, choose to know that you are being supported, held, and led by the presence of light within you. Take several deep breaths and trust that the Universe will cooperate with you when you cooperate with it. You are a team. Know it is your biggest fan, your greatest supporter, and the cheerleader of your soul.

"The Universe is my greatest supporter.

The Universe always has a better plan.

The power that created me is always working in my favor.

This I know and trust."

VIBE 13

Happiness is a gift to the world

Everything you do in this world moves out from you like a wave of energy. When you are kind, happy, and harmonious, this wave extends to all those who cross your path. And the kindness you share will eventually come back to you.

People always say, "What comes around goes around!" and they're often talking in terms of someone getting their just deserts, but the moment you get sucked into that energy is the moment you let the energy of fear and lack lead the way. Karma, the law of cause and effect, is ultimately a spiritual tool to encourage us to be kind and loving.

When you are kind to others, you are literally being kind to yourself too. When you focus on what makes you happy, it's as if the doors of your heart swing open and you move into the space of love that rests gently within. When you experience this love, you welcome all those around you into this space too. So, every time you experience bliss and joy, you are literally holding the space for others to experience it as well. Your happiness is a wave of healing for the whole world.

You were born to prosper.

You are here to shine.

Make it your purpose to share joy everywhere you go.

Have you ever noticed that when a day is going well and you're genuinely aligned to happiness, more and more reasons to feel blessed make themselves available to you?

Happiness creates a magnetic aura around you. Happiness attracts happiness.

Today you are encouraged to recognize all the simple things that make you feel happy. When you are happy, you raise your vibration and you allow others to raise their vibration too. Happiness is infectious. Think of it—when someone starts to smile, you can't take that smile off your own face, can you?

VIBE OF THE DAY

Today's exercise is simply smiling as much as you can. Offer the gift of joy to all those you meet.

Everywhere you go, look for the simple blessings that surround us all. Recognize that happiness is a gift and it's yours anytime you allow it to be.

"Happiness is a gift.
I am blessed with joy.
Every smile I share allows this gift to be shared.
Today I recognize the blessings in my world."

VIBE 14
Putting down roots

The base/root chakra is the seat of the kundalini energy, and the instinct of the kundalini is to rise up. In order for this to happen, it's important for its foundation to be strong. Imagine it being similar to well-primed soil in which seeds are planted: if the moisture and temperature are right, everything is in place for those seeds to begin germinating, putting down roots, and growing.

Your job is to do the same with your intentions and energy.

We've already mentioned that the base chakra governs your "backbone." That means that this space is all about feeling safe and having the courage to move forward in your life. That doesn't mean you have to be a roaring lion pouncing on every opportunity; it's about doing the inner work to have a strong and focused foundation.

That foundation, that soil, is your core ideas and beliefs. The seeds are new ideas. The roots are the manifestations of those ideas in your reality.

Activating your base chakra isn't only about putting down roots, though, but also about reclaiming your truth. It's about realizing and accepting that you have chosen to be here, upon this planet and in this life. It's about realizing that you weren't born to suffer, but to embody expansion, and the only way to do that is to take your power back into your own hands.

If you've been told that you're not safe, or that the Earth isn't safe, you have a huge opportunity to change this narrative.

What do you want to change it to?

What seeds are you ready to plant?

VIBE OF THE DAY

Are you ready and willing to reclaim your life?

It's time to know in your bones that you are safe on this planet. It's time to know that your body is the home of your soul. It's time to experience the world through the new truth that you have claimed for yourself.

Let this set of affirmations support you.

"I am at peace with myself."

"I am at peace with my body."

"I am at peace with the Earth."

"I recognize my strength."

"I am grateful for security."

"I completely accept that I have everything I need within me."

"I claim this as my truth."

Flow
(Sacral chakra)

The sacral chakra, the second chakra, is found at the center of the pelvis. In Sanskrit it is known as Svadisthana, "One's Own Place," and it is the chakra that governs the reproductive system and sexual organs. Ruled by the element of Water, on an emotional level its energy is expressed through our right to be in our own body, our capacity to flow with life, and our innate ability to create, both through reproduction and through our gifts. Traditionally, the sacral chakra is seen as a warm orange color.

When the sacral is in alignment, we'll have a strong sense of self-awareness and the ability to trust in the flow of life. Even if we're facing uncertainty or challenges, we'll trust in our own ability to find a way forward, knowing our gifts can see us through.

If there's lack of energy in this center, there's a good chance that on an emotional level there's a lack of trust in ourselves, whether that is expressed as a lack of faith in our own abilities or through our personal relationships and commitments.

On an energetic level, this center is where we focus energy in order to bring life to our projects and intentions.

If you want to bring healing and awareness to this space, it's important to forge a level of trust in your body, your gifts, and ultimately life itself. All of these concepts are explored in this section.

VIBE 15

Come home to your body

Have you noticed that it has become popular to be busy? We go around with full schedules and have grown used to being on the go.

There's nothing wrong with being busy, but when we get pulled into the vortex of activity, we can forget about our own needs and miss a lot of the messages our body and soul are sending us.

Have you allowed yourself to become addicted to being busy? Do you feel lost when your schedule for the day is empty? If the answer is "Yes," it's time to change that.

Have you ever noticed that if you've had a really busy few months, when you finally take a holiday, or even a day off, you get sick? That's your body making sure that you finally stop and take some time to be with yourself.

When you come back to your body, you come back to the clearest guidance system you have. When you give yourself the amazing gift of more time to really listen, you'll hear what your body wants you to know. If you take the time to check in with your body on a regular basis, you won't have to face a more intense signal from it when it needs your attention.

When you become more aware of the natural rhythms and messages of your body, you will become spiritually "embodied," and this deeper state of awareness will allow you to raise your vibration.

Your body is the home of your soul. Listen to it and learn how it can support you on your spiritual pathway.

VIBE OF THE DAY

Today you are encouraged to come back into your body. Take some time to give thanks for this amazing vehicle and the messages it sends you. Your body wants nothing more than to be happy and healthy, and if you really, really listen to it, it will tell you what it needs to be well.

"Today I choose to arrive within my body.

It feels so good to pick up the natural messages my body sends me.

Every cell of my being is blessed today because I am in touch with a deeper part of myself.

I am so grateful for the chance to know when my body needs my attention and love.

Every breath I take restores me in every way that is right for me.

I am embodied, connected, and in touch with who I truly am."

VIBE 16

Your passion is prosperous

You are so blessed to be in this world, because there are unlimited opportunities for you to learn and grow in your own unique way. The beauty of this world is the fact that we are all different and we all have our own interests. We all have something that we are passionate about. Passion is a natural energy that helps us express who we really are and share our gifts, talents, and creativity with the world.

Your passion can be something to do with your career or a hobby you are involved in. Whatever it is, it sets your soul on fire, helps you forget all your cares, and gives you space to be in the present moment, full of joy and contentment.

What's your passion? What do you love to do? When you choose to do what you love, you express yourself fully and become centered with your soul.

When you tune in to the vibration of passion, you also naturally draw the energy of prosperity toward you. Prosperity is the energy of fulfillment and riches.

Your truest form, your soul, is always in a place that is filled with support, abundance, and fulfillment. When you do what you love, you allow that sense of abundance to move into your body and mind and experience it on a physical level. Limitations in your mind begin to melt away and you're lifted so high on a vibrational level that you're in touch with the totality of possibility and you move onto a frequency that has unlimited support and potential for you.

That's the real definition of prosperity.

And prosperity is available to you right now, through your passion.

When you are pulsing with your passion, you align with the infinite heart of the Universe and you can manifest the life you love.

Experience your passion
+ Experience prosperity
= Raise your vibration

VIBE OF THE DAY

"It feels so good to do what I love.

When I experience my passion in life, I
am unbounded and limitless.

When I follow my passion, I attract and experience prosperity.

I move into the totality of possibility that surrounds me.

It feels so good to experience more of what I love.

And so it is!"

VIBE 17
Relationships are assignments

When you start to raise your vibration, you have a greater idea of who you are, what you have to offer, and what you'd like to experience. This brings so much clarity to the relationships you have in your life.

The deeper your spiritual exploration, the deeper your need will be for honest relationships. But it's important to know that in a spiritual sense, no relationship in your life is wrong. Every relationship is an assignment.

If there are people in your life you aren't fully resonating with, that's okay. Don't feel guilty. Not seeing eye to eye with someone doesn't make you (or them) any less (or more) spiritual.

When you realize a certain relationship isn't congruent with the rest of your path and you don't want to associate with that person anymore, you are listening to your soul. When you decide to let go of that relationship, you are honoring divine guidance.

If there's a relationship that you are ready to let go of, work on the most compassionate and appreciative way of doing that. Send the person love and gratitude for the relationship up to this point. Then imagine you are cutting all of the fearful and limiting cords to that person that are holding you both back.

In order to be more in your flow and to experience uplifting and fulfilling relationships, first of all be honest with yourself. What are you looking for? Then, if you're ready to connect with others who are coming from the same space as you, think about how you can make room for those connections in your life.

Today, give thanks for the relationships you love. Tell the people involved what you love about them, ask how you can support them, and be grateful for the positive and honest connection you have.

"All of the relationships in my life reflect honesty.

I am grateful for the people who love me.

It feels so good to know that I am clear in my relationships and that I support and feel supported in perfect balance.

Every relationship in my world is a divinely guided relationship.

Today I recognize the divine in myself and others."

VIBE 18
It's safe to have desires

"Desire" is a powerful word. It's an intense, fluid, and exciting word. It's not just a word either, it's a feeling, a sense of longing for something, someone, even a fantasy. There are a lot of false narratives running around in spirituality, telling us that desires are bad, but they're not, they're part of being human. You chose to incarnate as a human, and it's important to be fully human in order to become fully spiritual.

So, the most important thing for you to know right now is that you are allowed to have desires. It's okay to want things and it's okay to strive for something, especially if you're on the highest road possible.

When you have a desire for something, it's best to check it's a healthy desire, though. So, ask yourself why you want it. If it's because it's going to make you happy or a better person, then begin to move toward it.

Most people don't allow themselves to have desires because they feel they're being selfish. It's almost as though on some deep level they believe that if they have something, particularly something luxurious or expensive, they're depriving someone else of it. But in receiving something, we're bringing balance to the world.

Many of us feel that we're constantly giving. We can feel that we're giving so much of ourselves that there's nothing else to give. When we're receiving, the first thing that's happening is that we're redressing the balance. The second thing is that we're teaching those around us that they too can receive.

The Universe is happy to share its energy with us. And that energy never ceases to be, never runs out, and can never die. There is more than enough for everyone. Today, realize that there is no lack in the heart of the Creator and there is no need to have lack in your life.

When you decide to honor your desires, you give yourself permission to dance with the Universe and receive support on your path to growth and happiness.

VIBE OF THE DAY

You are encouraged to have a date with your desires today.

"Desire is a powerful emotion.

*I have recognized that I have needs and
I am finally honoring them.*

*It's okay for me to want some things from life,
because there's enough for everyone.*

In receiving, I bring balance to the world.

In manifesting, I show others that they can manifest too.

*I am grateful to be held by the Universe as it
meets my needs for the highest good of all."*

VIBE 19

Calling back the power of your pelvis

For hundreds of years, spirituality has been detached from sexuality. We've also been pushed by the mainstream media to detach from our sensual organs, to keep them covered or private. But deep down inside our pelvis, we hold the key to the Universe.

The sacral chakra is the sacred energetic space that is related to our reproductive system and our sensual organs. It represents our capacity to create.

This world itself was created through a gigantic vibration that brought life into being. It's no mistake, therefore, that the creation of human and other life is connected to the energy of orgasm, which is essentially a full-body vibration.

Religion and the media have made sexuality "unholy" not because it's unspiritual, but because it's so powerful. And they prefer to keep people "small" and "contained."

We have to reclaim this space as sacred. If you are holding a great deal of shame in your genitals, this needs to change. If you have encountered trauma in this space, this needs to heal. If you want to raise your vibration, it's important to establish a loving bond with your pelvis and genitals.

It's time to call back the power of your pelvis.

Your pelvis is your sacred place.

It is your connection to creativity.

It is your power center.

Reclaim what is yours.

- Send a seed of light from your heart into the sacred space inside your pelvis.

- Apologize to your genitals if you feel you've detached from them.

- Reclaim this space as sacred with the words below.

- Know that within you, you hold the sacred tools to connect to the vibrational frequency of creation. Know that your human body is an echo of what is happening in the heavens.

VIBE OF THE DAY

"Today I honor the sacredness of my body.

My sensual–sexual organs are a gift.

I reclaim my pelvis as my own.

This is my power center.

I hold the light of creation within me.

My body is holy.

And so it is."

VIBE 20
The fear of failure

"Failure" is something we never like to experience. It's something we fear and want to avoid. But in truth, failure is an illusion that the external world has created for us—and we decide if we fall into that nightmare or not.

It's time to tackle the old idea of failure so that you can surmount it once and for all.

In order to move beyond a limiting belief like failure, you have to understand how it was created in the first place. The truth is that failure is just one person's opinion of the outcome of a situation. When we say something is "a failure" or we've "failed," we're basically saying that something didn't turn out the way we hoped.

What if "failure" is just the Universe having a different plan? What if, when something goes "wrong," there's a bigger picture there? What if there's a better opportunity coming and if things had gone according to plan, you would have missed it?

Today you are encouraged to surrender your expectations. It's time to realize you can't actually let down the Universe, because the Universe has no expectations of you in the first place. You are encouraged to realize that failure is just a feeling, and that feeling is simply the acknowledgement that things didn't go the way you wanted. It doesn't mean things aren't going to be good.

This doesn't mean you can't acknowledge the *fear* of failure. Just don't let that be your story.

It's time to realize that whatever you focus on, you send energy to. So, when you fear failure, you are setting yourself up for it. When you're surrendering to the Universe, to that ultimate force of goodness, on the other hand, you're setting yourself up to experience goodness.

Failure can only exist for people who want control. So, to overcome the idea of failure, you are encouraged to surrender the idea of control.

You are reminded that you can never stray from your path to growth. You can never fail at being who you are.

Every experience in your life is a perfect
opportunity to know yourself at a deeper level.

VIBE OF THE DAY

"I realize that no external experience or
achievement can determine my worth.

I accept that I am always doing the best I can.

I honor myself and my journey.

I recognize how far I have come.

I know that I haven't lost my way because I have found myself."

VIBE 21
Trusting the flow

When it comes to planting seeds, there's a method. You prepare the soil, you plant the seeds, and you water them.

You trust that the seeds will grow because it is in their nature.

You trust that the seeds will grow because there is a method and a law.

For the seeds of your life to grow, there needs to be a level of trust that it is in their nature to grow.

That's what it means to trust the flow.

Life has a flow to it. It has the capacity to unwind and reveal each step in the perfect time–space sequence.

You were born to grow and you were born to flow.

You were born to flow because water is your essence. You were born from water, you are made of water, and you are sustained by it.

When things have been difficult or have gone wrong, it can be difficult to trust the flow. You put yourself in a cocoon of protection, maybe expecting the worst possible outcome, so that if things do go wrong, at least you are prepared.

But that isn't trust. That is fear.

You see, somewhere along the way, you learned that you have to fight for what you need and that you need to protect yourself from what can go wrong. But living a high-vibrational life isn't a battle, it's an opportunity to love and be loved.

Learning to trust the flow comes from learning to trust yourself. Your body is miraculous. Every day you defy the laws of nature and gravity just by being here. You are a walking miracle. But not only that: because you are here, you have a right to be here.

**You were born on purpose and
you can live with purpose.**

When you move into a state of trust within your body, you activate the sacral chakra, which supports your capacity to create a life in which you can trust *and* flow.

VIBE OF THE DAY

"I was born to flow.
It is in my nature to trust.
The power that created me created me on purpose.
I have a right to be here in my body.
My body is a miraculous vessel.
I hold life and light within.
I trust my body and I trust life."

IgNitE

Ignite
(Solar plexus chakra)

The solar plexus chakra, the third chakra, is found in the center of the body. In Sanskrit it is known as Manipura, "Lustrous Gem," and it governs the stomach, digestive system, central organs, middle back, and core muscles. Governed by the element of Fire, it is the central sun of the body and on an emotional level represents our willpower, drive, and intentions. Traditionally, it is seen as a bright yellow color, like the summer sun.

When our solar plexus is in alignment, we'll feel a fire within us that is warm and focused, giving us the capacity to fulfill our commitments and "make things happen." We'll also be able to trust our "gut feelings."

If there's a lack in energy in this center, there's a good chance that on an emotional level we'll feel out of control or that our life is out of our own hands. This may manifest as high levels of anxiety that may affect our digestive system or appetite.

On an energetic level, this center is the space that brings a creative fire to our goals and intentions.

If you want to bring healing and awareness to this chakra, you are guided to recognize that your life is your life! By recognizing that you have the power to assert your will and make your own decisions, you honor your free will and direct it accordingly. All of this is explored in this section.

VIBE 22
Within you is a mighty power

Within you is a mighty power. You have the ability to achieve your dreams and create miracles in your life. Everything you do and say is radiating out from you now and preparing the way. You are a limitless being, suspended in a Universe that is full, vibrant, and unlimited in energy. It's with you now, it's in you now, and it's got your back.

The power of intention is amazing. It's always working, even when you don't realize it. Everything that you say as a statement, sarcastic or not, is an intention. Every experience you accept into your life is also an intention. Now let me get this clear: I'm not telling you to stop having a laugh, but I am encouraging you to get clear about what you want to experience in the world.

Experiencing bad behavior from others or feeling abused or taken advantage of can affect our intentions. It's like this: if a friend, colleague, or partner starts to treat us in a way we don't feel is acceptable and we don't use our inner power to change it, the Universe (even though it doesn't want this for us) will start to echo this type of experience in all four corners of our life. It's as if magnetic waves from our thoughts and experiences move into our aura and attract similar energy, which then brings similar experiences into our life.

It's strangely easy to forget the fact that we are powerful and able to create amazing experiences, especially if life comes along and sweeps us up in a wave. A great tool that has helped me is being able to declare to the Universe whether I feel something is in alignment with what I am ready to receive or not. For example, if something happens that I would like more of, I say: "Yes, Universe, this is what I'm talking about—this is exactly the sort of experience I enjoy and am open to receiving!"

VIBE OF THE DAY

"I am grateful that I can cultivate my life.

Every thought and feeling I have is creating my world.

I am ready to clear all thoughts and intentions that are not aligned with my happiness.

Today I choose to know that only good experiences lie before me.

My life is a joy and I choose to experience joy in all four corners of my life.

It feels so good to be in tune with the field of energy that moves through me.

I am safe."

VIBE 23

Let inner fire warm you, not burn you

You are an inspired, spiritual, and exciting individual. You have been called to play a larger part in this Universe and you have responded to that call. You have learned that you have a light within you and you have recognized that you have divine inspiration moving through you at all times. Your inner fire motivates you, encourages you, and guides you.

But when we are receiving ideas and inspiration, it's very easy to get sucked into a task or a dream, pour all of our energy into it, and burn ourselves out. Also, if we're always trying to be in control of a situation and can't take a step back to review where we are right now, there's a chance we're blocking our dream from happening.

So, it's important to know the Universe always works on divine timing. It doesn't have any expectations of us, nor does it give us any time restrictions. We are all moving at the right pace for us, and you are encouraged to acknowledge that now.

> *The Universe and its angels want to support*
> *you and your dreams. So take a step back*
> *and allow this divine support in.*

Your angels of light are with you now and they want you to know that it's important to stay interested in your goals, but not to put so much of your energy into them that you end up feeling depleted. Draw on the support of the Universe and trust in its divine timing.

VIBE OF THE DAY

Today you are encouraged to take a step back and allow the Universe to meet you halfway. Recognize that whatever dream or goal you are working on is coming to fruition in its own good time and that over-possessiveness can end up holding you back rather than taking you forward.

Know that you have done what you need to and hand the rest over to the Universe. Know that angels are gladly taking over from here so you can be guided to your highest good.

"Today I hand this situation over to heaven.

I am grateful for the support that is all around me.

I trust that I am moving forward in a way that is for my greater good.

I allow the Universe to meet me halfway.

I am grateful for all of the steps I have taken and I honor them now.

I have given my all and now I step back to receive.

And so it is!"

VIBE 24
Making friends with your ego

The ego is the small voice within. It's the voice that tells us we're not good enough and our dreams aren't possible. It's the voice that sends our anxiety haywire.

The ego has a plan of its own. It likes to throw a curveball. It loves to tip us off-balance, and when it likes, it can be one nasty piece of work.

The best way to imagine the ego is to think of it as an unwanted houseguest. You know, the type that leaves a mess behind them and thinks of no one but themselves. Yep, it's basically that in mental form.

Having an ego is one of the requirements of being human. It comes with the mortal shell. It's a reminder of the limitations that exist within the physical realm.

But it's important to know that your ego isn't working *against* you. It's not evil. It's just acting the only way it knows how.

In fact, the ego has a purpose. I know it's hard to accept that, but it does. It writes a failure story to our success dreams not to hold us back, but to give us a choice. It thinks about the worst possible outcome not to limit us, but to help us decide what story we are going to allow to be our truth.

The ego is limited by the physical, but we are not.

You are a spiritual being within the physical world. Your truth is not limited by gravity.

When you're dealing with your unwanted houseguest, it can be easy to fight and bicker with it, but today you are encouraged to let that be your old story. For the moment that you fight with your ego is the moment you let your mental space become a battlefield. And your mind wasn't made for war, it was made for miracles.

**When you're challenged by your ego,
it's an opportunity to rise.**

Instead of fighting your ego, thank it for sharing its story and then choose your truth. Then you'll find you become one with your ego and fear is outweighed by love.

VIBE OF THE DAY

"Hello, ego, Thanks for being here and sharing your opinion.

*Today I am choosing my own truth and living
that miraculous story to the maximum.*

I realize that today is an opportunity to call back my power.

*Wherever love is present, fear is a stranger,
and love is here within me.*

I am love."

VIBE 25
Intuition integration

Your intuition is speaking to you every day and is available to you every moment. Every time you ask yourself a question, it sends an answer, prompt, or information to support you with whatever you are facing.

Listening to your intuition is like developing muscle strength—the more energy, focus, and exercise it is given, the stronger it will become. If you're like most of us, you most likely don't listen to yourself the majority of the time, and that's why it can be difficult to differentiate between intuition and ego.

Intuition and ego both communicate through inner dialogue, but there is a way to determine who's doing the talking. Just ask yourself, "How does this communication make me feel?"

If you feel safe, warm, or centered, it's love/intuition.

If you feel scared, overwhelmed, or anxious, it's fear/ego.

Another way to determine when the ego is running the show is if the information you are receiving has some sort of time limit or constraint, or even a promise that something will happen. For example, "If you don't do this now, something bad is going to happen in your future," or, "Buy this space and open a retreat— you'll become mega-rich!"

The ego has a promise—and it's always false. It never speaks in the present tense, but always about a situation in the past or something that may happen in the future.

The voice of intuition/love is different. When this voice speaks, it will instantly make you feel calm, warm, and centered. Even if all hell is breaking loose around you, love will hold you in a sacred cocoon and help you access the information you need in order to emerge from the darkness and into the light. Intuition/love isn't concerned about missing opportunities, for it knows that life is miraculous and more doors will open along the way. It trusts that everything is happening as it should.

The voice of love is as loud as your willingness to listen.

VIBE OF THE DAY

"Today I choose to listen to the voice of love.

Dearest intuition, I am willing to listen. Thank you for speaking loud and clear."

VIBE 26
Releasing shame

Shame is a real and raw emotion, often because it's repeating a story or a situation that is filled with regret, comparison, and judgment. But that story is often not the truth.

In order to bust through the blockages in your life and raise your vibration, it's important to face any stories you're telling yourself that are filled with humiliation and shame. I can tell you right now, their main theme will be feeling inadequate.

It's time to change the narrative.

There are always going to be things in life that we regret or wish we could change, and there are going to be various things about our life that we wouldn't like other people to know. But the reason you are here today, doing this work, is because you know that there is good within you. And there is. You are choosing to raise your vibration not just for yourself, but also because you know that you can positively contribute to the lives of those around you, and ultimately the world. You are more than good enough—you are great.

**The Universe sees you as filled
with unlimited potential.**

One way to release shame and move beyond it for good is to kick out the energy of comparison. You may be very used to this energy. You may have been compared to others by your parents, peers, colleagues, partners, and so on. Your ego may repeat these stories or replay these situations like a movie in your head. You may get sucked into the low feeling of shame because you didn't do the same thing as someone else, or "get it right," or because you weren't "perfect."

But the truth is different. The truth is:

There is no one like you. You are one of a kind.

**So there are no grounds for
comparison with anyone else.**

Don't let shame hold you down. Rise above it by removing comparison from your life once and for all.

VIBE OF THE DAY

"I am one of a kind.
I release the energy of comparison from my life.
When I release comparison, I release stories of shame.
I am one of a kind.
And I am worthy of love."

VIBE 27
Sharing trust

Trust is a big deal, especially these days. We've all had people lying to us and people lying about us. We've all endured betrayal.

To successfully raise your vibration, it's important to surround yourself with people who are honest, trustworthy, and loving. You need to be supported, you need to feel supported, and you also need to be a supportive supporter—in order to encounter trustworthy people, you yourself need to be trustworthy.

Both friendships and relationships require a balance of giving and receiving. Sure, sometimes you have to give more and at other times you will be more in need, but true relationships will balance out and outshine the rest.

Being able to be honest in all relationships is crucial, because if you can't be, you're not being who you truly are. When you're holding back from saying something or are unable to share a deeper aspect of yourself because you fear (or know) you'll be made a mockery of, or the information isn't safe with that person, it's time to change that.

Whatever is missing in your relationships, you are invited to bring that energy forth.

> **To be in good company, you have to be good company.**
>
> **If you are seeking honesty, you are invited to be honest.**
>
> **If you want to feel seen, you must be willing to see.**

So, support those you love. Give thanks for the relationships you have and ask yourself how you can be loving and supportive to those around you. Seek forgiveness where it is needed and offer support wherever you can in order to feel more supported.

VIBE OF THE DAY

Although today's task may not be done over 24 hours, it will enable you to feel more supported and balanced. It's to attract people you can trust and who can trust you. You can do this by being more aligned with who you are.

"My trustworthy spirit attracts and creates trusting relationships.

I offer support to others and experience support in return.

I am surrounded by relationships that reflect who I am.

I am a magnet to loving connections."

VIBE 28
Let your light shine

Within you is an incredible light, one that will never go out. Whenever you face darkness and uncertainty, that light has an opportunity to shine. It represents the greatest aspect of your being—the ancient you, the all-knowing you. It's the energetic representation of your soul.

The light of the soul is held within the solar plexus chakra. In order for it to shine as brightly as it can, you have to dial into and heal the energetic topics covered by that chakra.

Although there is a light within you, you'll know that at some of the most important times of your life, it has remained hidden. The best way to understand this is to liken your light to the sun on a cloudy day. You know the sun is up there and you know that it is shining, because that's what it does, but its warmth, brightness, and potency are out of sight. In order for it to be seen in all its glory, the clouds need to part. That's all. All the sun has to do is be itself.

The clouds in this metaphor are all of the stories of shame and inadequacy you've encountered along the way. Those stories, those clouds, aren't the truth, they are just stories that others have told you about yourself, often because they have been prevented from being themselves. You may have even repeated these stories to yourself.

It's time to change that.

The way to change it is to realize that these stories aren't challenges, but opportunities.

It's time to claim back your life and your right
to decide for yourself, now and forever.

VIBE OF THE DAY

"I reclaim my right to decide.
It is safe for me to make my own decisions and live my own life.
I choose to remove the clouds that hide my inner light.
I release the false narratives of shame and embarrassment.
My will is strong and focused.
My light is shining like the sun."

GIVE

AND

RECEiVE

Give and Receive
(Heart chakra)

The fourth chakra, found at the center of the chest, is the heart chakra. In Sanskrit it is known as Anahata, "the Unstruck," and it governs the heart and the surrounding anatomy, such as the diaphragm, upper ribcage, middle back, sternum, and shoulder blades. On an emotional level, the heart chakra governs all matters of the heart, including love, connections, and generosity. Ruled by the element of Air, this is the spiritual center that represents our capacity to love and be loved—to give and receive.

Traditionally, this chakra is seen as emerald green, but when we master the lessons of the heart, it reaches a higher, more ascended state called "the higher heart," which is pink.

When our heart chakra is in alignment, we'll find it easy to give generously and receive graciously. Even if we're going through a hard time, we'll trust that we deserve love and that everything is working out as it should.

If there's a lack of energy in this center, jealousy or selfishness can be expressed and there might be the concern that if we give, we will experience lack. For those who have previously endured heartache, there might also be the concern that love will never be possible.

If you want to bring healing and awareness to this chakra, you are guided to see that love isn't something you have to work for, but something you have to accept is inherently yours. All of the lessons in this section are dedicated to this.

VIBE 29

"No" to them, "yes" to you

Raising your vibration is about maintaining a sense of balance. It's about learning when to give and when to receive.

The truth is, we are wired to be kind and generous. It's in our nature to want to help those around us. If we give effortlessly, though, it can be difficult to shift into a state where we are being supported rather than constantly being the supporter.

So many people are walking this Earth giving every last drop of themselves until there is nothing left.

> **Learning how to receive is one of the most important aspects of raising your vibration.**

As someone who's here to change the world, you can teach others through your life and your boundaries. You may have been taught that "no" is not an answer, but I'm here to tell you that it is.

> **When you say "no" to others, you say "yes" to yourself.**
>
> **When you say "no" to others, you make space to receive.**

When you receive, you allow yourself to be replenished with all that you have given and more. And you *deserve* to be replenished, because just by existing you share so much with the world. Own this.

It's never easy to strike the balance between giving and receiving, but the truth is, you'll know when to take a time-out and when you really want to say "no." And when you say "no" to someone, even if it's someone you really love, you teach them to honor the needs of those around them.

By saying "no" to others, you also teach them that "no" is a full sentence and that it's an acceptable answer. By saying "no" to others, you give them permission to say "yes" to themselves.

VIBE OF THE DAY

Where in your life do you need to say "no," so that you can say "yes" to yourself?

If you need a hand saying "no" to a request, use this:

"I am sorry you are going through this. I want nothing but the best for you. You deserve to be happy. But right now I can't help you with that. So I'm going to have to say 'no' to you, so I can say 'yes' to myself. Thank you for understanding and respecting my boundaries."

And stick to your word.

"I say 'yes' to myself.
I meet all of my needs.
I say 'yes' to myself.
I set myself free."

VIBE 30
Make way for miracles

Are miracles happening in your life? I believe we are all entitled to them.

As we've seen, a miracle is a shift in perception—it's changing the way you think. It can be as simple as choosing a loving thought over one that's filled with fear.

Miracles occur as natural expressions of love. When they don't occur, something has gone wrong. You could be thinking positively and trying to stay focused on love, but at the same time not be able to understand how things could change.

You can't allow your mind to get in the way of your ability to manifest beautiful miracles in your life. You just have to create the space for them and let the Universe do the rest.

It's not about how big a miracle is, but
how much room you create for it.

VIBE OF THE DAY

Today you are encouraged to make space for the miracles you deserve. If there's a situation you know needs a miracle, take the first steps and then let the Universe meet you halfway. For your job is not to perform miracles, just to create the space for them to happen. Instead of trying to do the math and work out what has to happen next, feed the situation with love and then hand it over to the Universe and the angels of light that dance through the cosmos.

Send love to the areas of your life that need a miracle today and imagine them being held in the hand of your Creator.

Trust that the Universe is supporting you as you accept the miracles you deserve.

"Today I make way for miracles.

I recognize that it's not how big a miracle is that's important, but how much room I make for it.

I send love to all the situations in which I need support.

I allow myself to feel supported.

Miracles occur naturally and I welcome them with an open heart."

VIBE 31
Love yourself

Loving yourself is probably one of the more challenging aspects of raising your vibration. The reason this can be hard is because the ego likes to challenge you on it. Every time you move into a more loving space, the ego will create its own plan or tell you what you don't want to hear.

The ego, as we learned a few lessons ago, is just doing its job. It's giving you the opportunity to trust what you know to be true. But it's time to go beyond what you've sabotaged yourself with in the past.

Loving yourself means truly honoring who you are. It doesn't always mean looking in the mirror and telling yourself, "I love you!" It can also be about the decisions you make in your life. Here are some examples:

- Not allowing others to treat you badly.

- Giving yourself time to do the things you love.

- Moving into a state of forgiveness with others because it removes the toxicity from within you.

Through self-love, realize that you are able to draw more universal light into yourself and raise your vibration to its optimum strength. Your ability to love yourself and respect who you are will become a healing wave that inspires those around you.

VIBE OF THE DAY

*"Today I choose to love myself enough to say
'no' to bad behavior or toxic emotions and make
room in myself to be nourished by light.*

*I realize that how I see myself has everything
to do with how the world sees me.*

*I choose to look at myself in a loving way and allow that
loving wave to wash from me and throughout the world.*

*Today I love myself enough to make the changes
I need to feel loved and accepted."*

VIBE 32
Give generously, receive graciously

The Universe is all about balance. You've heard about it already. People call it "karma" or "the law of cause and effect." We've mentioned already that karma is the law that encourages us to be kind. And as we give out kindness, it comes back and kisses us.

Giving and receiving works like this too. When we give, we are making room in our life to receive. When we give to others graciously and without expectation, the Universe needs to give to us. It's so simple, but we find it hard to accept.

The heart chakra represents kindness and altruism. It's the part of us that wants to share with those we feel are in need. When we give graciously, our heart chakra opens up and shines brightly.

You know how good it is to give someone a gift that you've put a lot of thought into and to see them enjoy it. You know how good it is to help someone out, even if it's just offering a hand to someone struggling to get their luggage down the steps at the train station. It feels good to give.

But when we give too much, our heart chakra can become drained. When this happens, we'll get frustrated at ourselves and feel that we can't give anymore. In order to maintain a sense of balance in our life, it is our spiritual duty to receive. Today you are being encouraged to do just that.

VIBE OF THE DAY

You are encouraged to let the Universe know that you are willing to receive. Welcome offers of help, support, and kindness into your life. If someone at work offers you a hand, accept it. If someone offers to cook you dinner or lunch, welcome it! If someone gives you a compliment, receive it and honor yourself.

Smile. Breathe. Receive.

"I am willing to receive.
I have recognized that I am deserving of love and support.
It feels good to give and it feels great to receive.
Today I welcome the energy of balance into my life.
My heart is open to receive."

VIBE 33

Forgiveness is a gift

When you come across the word "forgiveness," there's a good chance a past or present situation will make itself known to you. There's a reason for this: it's because you know forgiveness is something you need, but it's something you may be resisting too.

Forgiveness is a complex process. It's isn't easy to explain or experience, but it is certainly required in order to raise your vibration. It can mean something different to everyone, but for me it's ultimately no longer allowing a past situation to affect your current happiness.

Forgiving doesn't mean forgetting—it's more about saying that a situation happened, but it's not who or where you are today. In some ways, it's like looking at an old photograph. It may be in black and white, not color, and when you're looking back at yourself, that person doesn't feel like you anymore.

If there's something in your life that you know needs forgiveness but you're resisting, know this could be for a number of reasons. It could be because there's a part of you that feels the person you will have to forgive doesn't deserve it.

Let me tell you this: forgiveness isn't about whether someone deserves it or not. The point is that when you don't forgive, the only person that is suffering is you. It's painful and draining to hold on to the troubles of the past.

Don't let someone else's errors block your happiness.
Clear them from your vibration once and for all.

If you are holding back from forgiving *yourself*, realize that you would never know what you know today if you hadn't made those mistakes. Realize that you are a completely different person from who you were then. Now you are working on living with purpose and making a difference. You deserve to be free.

Forgiveness is an organic process. To experience it, all you have to be is willing, and the rest will take care of itself.

VIBE OF THE DAY

"Dear Universe,

I am willing to forgive.

I am willing to be forgiven.

Thank you for showing me the miracle of forgiveness.

I realize that forgiveness doesn't mean forgetting, but choosing love instead.

I welcome this freedom into my heart.

And so it is."

VIBE 34
Believing is receiving

You've probably heard, or even said, "I'll believe it when I see it." It's a common saying, but it's not how miracles work.

Believing is receiving.

You'll see it when you believe it.

Try believing that whatever you need in life, it's possible for you to have it. It *is* possible. Why?

You are unlimited in your capacity to create, because you are the Universe. Your body is made up of the particles of former stars. Every strand and cell of your being is in touch with the everything that is, was, and ever will be, and so you are the embodiment of pure potential. *Unlimited* potential, because the Universe is unlimited in its capacity to share and create. So everything you want is available to you now. Just believing this opens up the floodgates to miracles.

Your life is an opportunity to create the miraculous, and through experiencing the miraculous, you send waves of healing to old wounds, while demonstrating to future generations what is possible.

What message do you want to leave behind for future generations? What new pathways are you ready to forge? What miracles are you ready to receive?

VIBE OF THE DAY

Whatever you are seeking is within you now. Embody this and call forth all the miracles you require.

"My life is a manifestation of my beliefs, thoughts, and feelings.

I know that miracles are my birthright.

I am capable of manifesting miracles because I am a miracle.

I am pure potential manifest.

I receive what I believe.

I am ready for miracles.

And so it is."

VIBE 35
Higher purpose

Living with purpose means living in a way that offers service and meaning to the world.

It can be tricky to navigate.

A lot of us feel under pressure to live purposefully but often find it difficult to truly understand or embody what that means.

First of all, it's important for you to know that your life purpose is not your job title or the gifts that you have. It cannot be found on a business card or in a careers office. Your life purpose is not what you do for a living.

Your life purpose is to be happy.

That might feel far too simple, but it's the truth. When you're happy, you're contented, and when you're contented, you want to share, and when you share, you're living with purpose.

Your life choices, including your relationships, your hobbies, and even your career, can support your life purpose, but they don't define it, or you.

You are not what you do for a living.

You are not what it says on your business card.

You are not what you did or didn't study.

You are love.

You are love in action, and you may even have said a prayer like: "God, use me."

I'm here to invite you to upgrade this way of thinking. I know there's a better way, because for a long time that was my prayer, and for a long time I felt used.

So, instead of asking God/the Universe to use you, invite it to show you how you can be of service in a way that serves you, and even your bank account.

You see, it is possible for you to be served while you serve.

You can be sustained while you live with purpose.

The Universe is grateful for your commitment to the work.

VIBE OF THE DAY

Here's a prayer to support you:

*"Thank you, Universe, for showing me how I can
serve and live with purpose in a way that serves me,
my joy, my happiness, and my bank account.*

I feel so grateful to be living a life that is sustained by my service.

*I feel so grateful to know that my purpose is to be happy
and that when I am happy, I share my joy with the world.*

I am filled with purpose and I share it with the world.

And so it is."

EXPRESS

Express
(Throat chakra)

The throat chakra, the fifth chakra, is found at the bottom of the throat between the collarbones, tunneling through to the nape of the neck. In Sanskrit it is known as Vishuddha, "Command," and it is the chakra that governs the neck, the tops of the shoulders, the throat, mouth, tongue, and teeth. On an emotional level, it represents our truth and our capacity to express ourselves. Its element, which it shares with the next chakra, is Space, or Akasha in the Sanskrit traditions. Traditionally, when in balance, this chakra is blue in color.

When the throat chakra is in alignment, speaking up comes naturally to us. Even in times of high stress or overwhelm, we'll find the power to get our point across in order to care for our mental and emotional wellbeing.

If there's a lack of energy in this center, there's a good chance that emotionally we'll have a lump in our throat or find it difficult to express who we are or how we feel.

If you want to bring healing and awareness to this chakra, you are guided to speak up and unapologetically be who you were born to be. All of the lessons in this section are dedicated to this.

VIBE 36
Let truth be your teacher

It's not always easy to say what you want to say, especially if you're worried you're going to upset someone or let them down. Speaking your truth, either by revealing information to set yourself free, or telling someone how you really feel, or doing something you know you need to do, is a huge spiritual lesson. It's the moment you step into your power and allow your spiritual energy to expand.

If you're hitting brick walls or feeling your next step or the next phase of your life isn't clear, there's a good chance the Universe is asking you for more clarity. You see, you can be asking for one thing in your mind but acting out a different reality in your life. For example, if you're asking the Universe to show you how you can live in a more purposeful way, yet you're harboring old emotions and withholding your truth, then you're giving out mixed signals.

When you want to raise your vibration, you need to let your entire life reflect the energy you want to create. That includes how you communicate to others (and yourself).

Truth and integrity are some of the highest vibrations possible. Often we hold back with truth because we're concerned that it may be upsetting or hard for others to accept. But when we don't reveal our truth, we prolong an internal psychic pain that stops our wings from unfurling, when in reality our destiny is to soar. When we withhold the truth from others, we stop them seeing our light, when in reality we were born to shine.

Truth has called you here today and it's inviting you to reveal your whole self.

If you know you have something to say, it's time to make some space in your life to say it.

If you're worried about what's going to happen after that, then you must know that the Universe always has a better plan for you. When you make the first move, the Universe will present the next one to you.

Owning your truth is a spiritual assignment. To live a high-vibe life, your entire self needs to be aligned with authenticity and integrity.

You are here to embody your truth.

When you do so, the light of your true self is seen.

VIBE OF THE DAY

"I let my truth be my teacher.
When I share how I feel, the path ahead becomes clear.
When I reveal my truth, I allow myself to be seen.
I choose to be seen and heard.
I step into the light of my true self."

VIBE 37
Express your emotions

When we begin to live in a more truthful and embodied way, old energies, in the form of emotions, often rise up to be released.

Expressing these emotions isn't always the easiest thing to do, for it requires us to drop all the shields that we've built up and become completely vulnerable.

The reason we've put up the shields is because from an early age we've been told that being emotional is weak or disruptive. You know when a baby starts crying in public, the parent will often say, "Shhh," to them. Of course, that's meant to be soothing, but it's also saying, "Be quiet, this is disrupting the peace of those around you."

We carry that with us and later on we are taught: "If you need to cry, go outside," because being emotional just isn't socially acceptable.

Any of this sound familiar?

But if we don't express the energy of our emotions, we allow our pathway to be clogged up. On the other hand, when we release that energy, we create space in our life for positivity and blessings.

Wherever you are holding back emotionally,
you are holding yourself back, and you
know you deserve to be free.

The Universe is encouraging you to express your emotions with grace. If there's something you haven't released because you've been concerned about being perceived as weak, know that through your truthful expression you will tap into a spiritual strength.

Also, when you express yourself openly and honestly, you begin to drop the shields around your heart and allow yourself to be fully seen. When you step into this vulnerable space, you allow the love of your true self to emerge.

The only shield you need is your soul.

VIBE OF THE DAY

If you're unsure where to start with expressing your emotions, ask the Universe for help. It will guide you to authentically express who you are and how you feel.

"Thank you, Universe, for supporting me at this time. I hand over this entire situation to you.

Thank you for directing me in ways that I can recognize so that I can express my true feelings. It feels good to be honest with myself and those I love.

I am ready to express my whole self. I release the old and make space for the new."

VIBE 38
Talking to Source

The more clearly we communicate on Earth with our friends, lovers, and families, the more clearly we are able to communicate with the Universe. There's a synergy between how we navigate through this realm and what happens when we reach beyond the veil.

When we communicate with the Universe, we may imagine we're connecting to something "up there" in the sky or in a world beyond this, but the Universe is all around us and within us. I like to imagine that the heart is a stargate and through it we can reach heaven. With practice, it can become like a walkie-talkie that we can use to develop a personal relationship with the Source of creation.

Having a loving, open, and insightful conversation with Source can become a wonderful way of accessing support and comfort. When we really open up about our feelings, thoughts, worries, and decisions, we really give that divine presence the space to enter our life and support us.

You deserve to be supported.

But the Universe honors your free will, so before it can intervene, it needs your permission. You see, this is *your* life and these are *your* lessons. Until *you* decide you need an intervention, the Universe will support but not interject.

If you need an intervention or you would like more support, invite in all the help you need. Just by communicating what you need, or how you would like to feel, you are sending a clear signal to the Universe that you would like its help.

It doesn't matter how you see the Universe—it could be in the form of a particular saint, ascended master, angel, or deity, or even the cosmos—just know that it is ready and willing to listen to you.

VIBE OF THE DAY

The Universe is always more willing to help you than you are to be helped. It's time to open up and recognize that the divine is your greatest love, your best ally, and your truest friend. Speak to it. Share your concerns, reveal your feelings, let out your emotions, and breathe with ease.

"Dear Universe,

I am grateful for your love and support.

Thank you for hearing me clearly at this time.

Thank you for placing your hands of light on the areas of life where I have concerns.

I welcome your miracles now.

I know you are my greatest ally.

I accept your love and support now.

Thank you, thank you, thank you!"

VIBE 39
Your soul has a voice

The Universe is guiding you through the voice of your soul.

Your soul is the ancient you—the part of you that was never born, therefore will never die. It's the you that will continue on when your physical shell comes to an end, the you that has walked the Earth many times before this incarnation.

That ancient you has never left what we like to call heaven. It's multi-dimensional, so even though you are having a human experience, there's still a facet of your being in the heart of the Universe.

As you are an expression of the Universe, universal intelligence is available to you in every moment. The realization that this information is actually within you gives you the opportunity to unlock it.

Developing a connection to universal intelligence means developing a relationship with the voice of your soul. Hearing your soul is about acknowledging all the feelings and emotions and conversations that arise within you.

Through listening to yourself and being able to identify your ego, you will be able to identify when your soul is doing the talking.

The soul's voice is timeless and therefore always fixed on the present. It is not attached to any outcome, it has no material needs or desire for gain, but always trusts that good is unfolding.

The best way to nurture your connection to your soul is to create regular space for it to talk to you. Instead of asking about a particular situation or asking a question, give it space to speak up and share what it feels you need to know.

When you regularly listen to your soul, you open up to the unlimited support of universal intelligence.

VIBE OF THE DAY

Use this prayer to tune in to your soul:

"Divine voice of my soul, thank you for revealing to me what I need to know. I am willing to listen."

Then spend time listening.

"The Universe guides me through the voice of my soul."

VIBE 40
Get clear with Source

If you're encountering any stagnancy in your life, there's a good chance that you aren't being clear with the Universe.

The Universe is always listening, and not just listening to what you're saying to it, but also to what you're saying to yourself and others. All those little comments about yourself and your life are energy. All those comments are intentions that you are sending out to the Universe.

It's a tendency, for some reason, for humans to put themselves down. You know when someone tells you that you look lovely and you deflect the compliment? Or you're squeezing by someone and say, "Excuse my fat ass!" Do you want that to be your truth?

It might be that you don't even realize you're doing it, but let me tell you now, no one wants to hear you talk negatively about yourself or to yourself, even if you do it for a gag or at the time it's funny. The people around you love you and want nothing but the best for you.

The Universe wants nothing but the best for you.

It's time to ditch the negative comments about yourself, for they are confusing to the Universe. It's time to begin getting clear with the Universe, and the way you do that isn't just through your inner work, but through your whole life, including what you say to yourself.

You are here now because deep down you know you deserve healing.

So, every time you slip back into your old way of being, change the energy instantly by saying something like: "I clear, cancel, and release this statement. My truth is that I am whole, healed, and complete."

The more you get into the habit of doing this, the easier it will become for you to embody the change you are ready to create.

When you create consistency in your self-talk, out and in, this will become your reality.

VIBE OF THE DAY

"The Universe is always listening.
I welcome love, healing, and support into my world.
I choose to love and support myself.
The life I want is here. I choose to live it now!"

VIBE 41
The vibration of sound

Sound is a powerful tool, for when we create or connect with it, we are in touch with the energy of vibration. When an object vibrates, it causes movement in the molecules around it, causing them to bump into each other, which makes them vibrate too, and this reaction is what creates sound.

Sound clearly creates a physical shift within the body. When I learned that the human heartbeat mirrored the tempo of music, I wasn't surprised, for vibration is the language of the Universe. When we tune in to sound, we connect with the energy of creation, and when we make certain sounds, we stimulate dormant spiritual energies within that can support us along the way.

Making certain sounds, in particular the ones below, is also known to stimulate the vagus nerve, which is the longest cranial nerve in the body and critical for supplying information to the respiratory and digestive systems while maintaining control of the heart rate. Many holistic health practitioners believe it's the key to our wellbeing.

According to many Eastern belief systems, in the beginning there was a sound that stimulated creation. The idea is similar to what scientists call the Big Bang, because essentially that ginormous explosion in the heart of the Universe was a vibration that exploded with unimaginable force, creating matter and forcing it outward to create billions of galaxies.

The sound of creation was "Om" (in the Hindu tradition), also spelled as "Aum," or "Hum" (Buddhist), or "Ong" (Kundalini yoga), but some people also connect with the energy of "Ah," like a sigh of relief, and "Hmmm," like a buzzing bee.

The ancient masters and yogis knew that when they connected with sound, they connected with the pure divine energy of creation, and so they began to use chanting in their spiritual practice and thus were led to spiritual liberation.

When you chant or consciously make sound, you connect with the infinite potential of the Universe and build up the power to create. You remember your divine origins and are reminded that anything is possible.

You are invited to connect to the vibration of sound to unlock the power of the Universe within.

VIBE OF THE DAY

Take a deep breath and on your out-breath make each of these sounds. Hold each one for as long as possible. Close your eyes and feel the energy.

"OMMMMMMMMMMMMMMMM."

"AUUUUUUUUUMMMMMMMMM."

"HUMMMMMMMMMMMMMMMM."

"ONNNNGGGGGGGGGGGGGG."

"AHHHHHHHHHHHHHHHHHHH."

"HMMMMMMMMMMMMMMMMMM."

"When I connect with sound, I connect with the vibrational Source of creation.

When I embody sound, I unlock my power to create.

When I chant, I am united with the Oneness of the Universe."

VIBE 42

Shedding the weight of the world

The world can be an intense place to be. With all of the emotions, expectations, and even politics going on, sometimes it can feel impossible not to be weighed down by it all. Not to mention all of the expectation and pressure that's placed on you personally.

A lot of pressure can come with walking the spiritual path. People's opinions of you can change, and their expectations. Sometimes there's the expectation that you'll find the answer to every problem. That is heavy.

Not only that, but all of the energies of your past and all of the expectations of your parents, peers, and other people can weigh you down on a psychic level.

The throat chakra governs the space around the shoulders and neck, and this is where we carry the weight of the world. It may be expressed as bad posture or extremely tense shoulders.

Whether you are experiencing physical constraints or not, there's a good chance that you are carrying psychic pain.

In order for pure primal life-force to reach and activate the throat center, it's essential to clear all the weight, expectation, and pressure that are not yours to carry. You might be here to live a life of purpose, but you aren't responsible for the whole world. Taking on too much responsibility actually blocks your path to purpose.

There's a good chance that up to now, you didn't realize you had a choice. You may have empathically or compassionately felt helpless in certain situations and tried to alleviate the stress or pain of others by taking it on yourself.

But you can choose to release this energy for good.

VIBE OF THE DAY

"Thank you, Universe, for clearing from my energy the psychic pain that is not mine to carry. Thank you for removing the old stories, narratives, blockages, expectations, judgments, projections, plans, fears, concerns, and limitations that are not mine to carry.

I take the weight of the world off my shoulders.

I free up the space around my neck, shoulders, and back.

I am safe and free to express who I truly am.

And so it is."

See
(Brow chakra)

The brow chakra, also known as the third eye chakra, is found at the center of the forehead and runs all the way through to the rear of the skull. In Sanskrit it is known as Ajna, "Perception." It is the chakra that governs the eyes, head space, and frontal lobes of the brain. On an emotional level, it governs the mind—the energetic space between body and soul—and our capacity to "see." Its element is Space, Akasha. Traditionally, the energy of the brow is seen as indigo blue.

When the brow chakra is in alignment, we can see beyond limitations, have a clear vision, and feel our mind is a good friend.

If there's a lack of energy in this center, there's a good chance we aren't "seeing clearly" or are creating false narratives in our mind. Energetically, we may be haunted by nightmare thoughts or even have nightmares when we are sleeping.

If you want to bring healing and awareness to this chakra, it's important to recognize that the mind is a space that can be curated with love, and through perception, everything can be changed. All of the lessons in this section are dedicated to this chakra.

VIBE 43
Mindful, not mindless

Our mind is a magical space, for it's the space that allows us to access the information that's held in our brain, our body, and our spirit. It's also the space that allows us to develop a relationship with the Universe, set our intentions, and receive guidance.

The key to tapping into divine guidance is through the practice of meditation. In order to hear the Universe, you first have to listen to yourself.

There's a false idea that through meditation we are supposed to either control our mind or even switch it off. I think a huge part of this is because when we see meditation in the media, we are shown images of blissful monks or folks with unwrinkled faces smiling in meditation on the beach, and so on. This false narrative is then picked up by those seeking a more spiritually aligned life and it comes into their spiritual practice with them, creating what can only be described as unachievable expectations and thus creating a block in the development of their meditation practice.

Meditation isn't about switching off the mind, but giving it permission to switch on. That's why it's often referred to as "mindfulness," as the mind is full rather than empty.

Meditation is also about listening, observing, and accepting what is, rather than trying to fight or control it. Remember, the moment you try to control or even fight your mind is the moment you allow your mental space to become a battlefield instead of a space for miracles.

Of course, when you begin to develop your spiritual practice, you can also introduce tools that help you focus your mind, rather than control it, and through focused practices you have an opportunity to be liberated from the other stuff, but first you have to face it—you have to observe, listen, and connect with the energy, information, and maybe even the fears that are permeating your being.

Learn to sit, learn to observe, learn to listen, and the voice of the Universe will become more apparent to you.

VIBE OF THE DAY

"I take the time to listen to my inner voice.
My meditation practice is the opportunity to listen to myself.
When I listen to myself, I can hear the Universe.
I am willing to listen."

VIBE 44
Meeting Mara

There's an old story about the Buddha that can be so helpful when it comes to understanding how to face fear and overcome it. It's important to say the Buddha was just a normal human being who dedicated his time and energy to the elevation of his thinking and became enlightened. This is achievable for everyone.

The story goes that the Buddha was meditating in a cave one day and one of his devotees was standing at the entrance, keeping watch so that the Buddha could remain undisturbed. After a while, he noticed Mara coming up the hill toward him. Mara was a scary demon with multiple eyes, garlic breath, and a crown of skulls.

The devotee thought, *Shall I say, "The Buddha is out for lunch," or "The Buddha isn't here today"?* but before he knew it, he was face to face with the demon.

"I'm here to see the Buddha," Mara announced.

Before the devotee could say anything, from inside the cave the Buddha said, "Let him in."

Mara charged in.

The Buddha looked him straight in the eye and said, "I see you, Mara."

The Earth started to shake and Mara disappeared.

This story is a powerful metaphor:

- The cave is you.

- The devotee out front is your ego.

- The Buddha is your inner teacher.

- Mara is your greatest fear or your "demons."

You see, the ego, out front, wants you to be scared of the prospect of experiencing fear. That's often what creates the greatest anxiety when it comes to navigating fear—the "what if" rather than the experience of fear itself. As long as your fears are in the "what if" space, they will continue to have power over you.

But if, like the Buddha, you let fear "in" by seeing it for what it is, it will no longer be separate from you and therefore no longer able to have power over you.

VIBE OF THE DAY

"I see you, fear.

I no longer allow the prospect of experiencing you to have power over me.

I am one with all that is."

VIBE 45

I am willing to see this differently

Everyone has a story that they're telling themselves. But whether that story is true is another story.

When you begin to raise your vibration, there's a process of undoing. It's like an onion: the sweet spot is at the very core, and to get there, you have to peel away all the layers.

Within you is that same sweet spot. When you begin your spiritual practice, you begin to peel away all the layers that have built up to protect that spot. In this case, the layers are all the old energies and narratives you've picked up along the way. They could have started in childhood and more may have come in later through challenging experiences or relationships.

These layers are psychic pain that your energy field will begin to release when it knows that it doesn't have to protect itself anymore. As the layers peel away, there are often opportunities to revisit old stagnant energy, and although your current life may be vastly different from your past, the stories may be the same—stories that make you feel that you're not good enough, not lovable, talented, creative, or whatever it may be, stories that repeat the insulting behavior of people who were hurting you because they were hurting themselves.

There's a good chance that right now you're telling yourself a story that isn't true. It could be to do with a relationship with a family member or a partner. You could be telling yourself that they're thinking a specific way about you. You could be telling yourself that they're mad at you, or annoyed, or resentful.

It could be to do with your career. You could be telling yourself you haven't been working hard enough or that your boss doesn't think you're good enough at what you do.

These stories may or may not be the truth, but they *are* what you are telling yourself.

It's time to change that.

VIBE OF THE DAY

Whenever your ego begins to lead you down a dark path of self-loathing, you can simply set an intention to shift this reality. Every time you're making up a painful story, say:

"I am willing to shift my perception.

I release all false narratives.

I am willing to experience the truth.

Thank you, Universe, for helping me see this differently.

I am willing to see this differently."

VIBE 46
Clear seeing

Clairvoyance is the ability to "see" spiritually. For the most part, it is the ability to see into the future, to see spiritual beings, or even to see the truth of a situation before it's revealed. This spiritual vision isn't about seeing with our physical eyes, but about awakening the eye of our mind, the "third eye."

Throughout our life, our third eye will open and close. It's usually active when we are young, for when we are a child, we have fewer ego constraints. The ego doesn't want us to be spiritually connected, because when we begin to awaken on that level, it has less capacity to control us.

But it's our divine right to see on a spiritual level, for our essence is spirit. When we awaken our spiritual ability "to see," we begin to witness the world through the eyes of our original self.

There may be a part of you that is excited about this and another part of you that is hesitant, or even scared. It could be that you've seen movies or television series that have made someone having a spiritual experience seem scary, or maybe you're recovering from a religious upbringing that condemned your natural spiritual abilities as "unholy."

These are just ways to keep us small and leave the power in someone else's hands. Mainstream society doesn't want us to be powerful and gifted, because then it can no longer control us with scarcity and fear. Mainstream religions don't want us to have our own direct connection to Source, because we'll put them out of business.

So, when fears of spiritual sight begin to show up, it's not because you're scared of having a spiritual experience or scared of seeing a divine being. What you're really feeling is uncertainty: *Am I ready to be this powerful?*

Well, are you?

VIBE OF THE DAY

"I call back the power of my vision.
I am willing to see.
I call back my spiritual gifts.
I open the eyes of my spirit.
I was born to be this powerful."

VIBE 47
Angel eyes

I have a special phrase and it's really simple:

"In order to see angels, you have to be an angel!"

It's not always easy. But I believe that it is through being kind, generous, and supportive of others that we are able to perceive angels and understand them on a deeper level.

Angels are expressions of Source. The best way to understand them is to think of them as the thoughts of the divine. Therefore when we connect with the angelic realm, we are in direct connection with the mind of creation.

Everyone has angels around them.

You have angels around you now.

Angels want nothing more than for us to be happy and supported. They want the whole of humanity to understand that no matter what their race, creed, or color, they are all divine and all equal.

Angels see us as equal, but they also see us for who we truly are— they see our soul or spirit, the eternal source of love within us. We don't always see it, either in ourselves or in others, especially if they are being challenging or difficult. We don't always see the best in others either, particularly in strangers, because we don't know them and aren't looking for their light.

Angels, on the other hand, see the good in all. They see the soul in all of humanity. They always look for our loving essence and they encourage us to embrace it.

From the moment you were born your angel has seen your light and been waiting for you to discover it. When you see that light in yourself and then in others too, you are awakening your sacred vision and holding the space for others to discover their own miraculous light.

VIBE OF THE DAY

If you are ready to awaken your inner vision, you must raise the vibration of your vision. So today you are encouraged to see through the eyes of angels.

Wherever you are, wherever you go, and whatever you do today, acknowledge that everyone you see, no matter who they are or what they are doing, has a soul within them and that soul is ready to light up.

If you can see that light, their energy will vibrate at a higher level and you yourself will move into a space that is wise, compassionate, and loving.

"I choose to see through the eyes of angels.

In every person I meet or see, I have the opportunity to witness love.

Will you enter into my vision, holy thoughts of Source?

Through the eyes of angels, I see the world.

I am willing to see the love in all.

I am willing to see love."

VIBE 48

My mind is an altar to Source

Everything you hold in your mind is what you hold up to the Universe. Your mind is an altar to Source.

Your mind is a space of power.

There's a good chance, however, that there are certain things in your life, or in your mind, that are disturbing you. They could be memories of your past or concerns about your future. You could be trying to figure out how it's going to unfold, just in case you need to protect yourself.

You may find yourself praying for healing, or a miracle, or resolution, in the hope that the future will deliver the answer. But there's no place more powerful than now. And the Universe is present in everything.

The Universe is present in the situations that cause you pain.

The Universe is present in the situations that cause you concern.

Everything in the Universe is one, and therefore everything you're worried about has the opportunity to receive universal support.

The way you welcome in help is by reminding yourself that nothing is separate from Source and by placing your concern into the hands of the Universe.

When you give something back over to the Universe, you remind yourself that no matter what is happening, you are never alone.

Through the Universe, you are connected to the energy of creation, miracles, and unconditional love.

Hand your worries over and let the Universe take the wheel.

VIBE OF THE DAY

"My mind is an altar to Source.

On this altar, I place all the situations that concern me.

I know the Universe is with me and within me.

In every moment, every concern, every challenge,
I have the opportunity to be supported.

I welcome in the support of the Universe
and thus I welcome in miracles.

Thank you, Universe, for leading the way."

VIBE 49

I am seen

The brow or third eye chakra is said to be the most sacred of all the energy centers in the body, for this is where the kundalini climbs to in what can only be described as a crescendo moment, when this chakra is activated, supporting the opening of the crown chakra and initiating the direct experience of Source.

When our third eye opens, our entire view of the world shifts. Everything we thought we knew, everything we understood and believed, can be altered in a single experience.

Once we've had this "eye-opening" moment, we may want to keep our third eye open. In fact this is one of the motivations for raising our vibration. We can create a clear vision that allows us to see beyond this dimension and gain deeper clarity about our way forward. But there's a critical piece of information that is often missed: opening our third eye isn't only about being able to see, it's about allowing ourselves to be seen.

You see (!), when we have a spiritual awakening, we reach a state of heightened vulnerability and all of the psychic shields that we've built up over our journey come tumbling down.

Psychic shields are shields that our own psyche has erected because, through our past experiences and sensitivity, we've learned that we can be hurt, and we want to protect ourselves from it happening again.

But let me tell you, those shields are not only draining, they are preventing you from being fully seen by the Universe.

Don't get this confused: the Universe can see you, but you're not allowing yourself to be seen.

If you are ready to see the world from a higher perspective, you must choose to be fully seen. To be seen, you need to drop the psychic shields of pain, for the only shield you need is love.

VIBE OF THE DAY

"I am willing to be seen.
I drop the psychic shields that are blocking my view.
I am willing to be seen as my whole self.
Thank you, Universe, for healing my vision.
I awaken from the dream. I can see and I am seen."

Know
(Crown chakra)

The crown chakra, the seventh chakra, is found at the top of the head. In Sanskrit it is known as Sahasrara, "Thousand-petaled," and is seen as a lotus with 1,000 petals. It governs the top of the head, the brain, and the hair. On an emotional level, it governs our connection to Source—both our beliefs and our experience of what we call "God." Traditionally, the colors of the crown are violet and crystal clear, and the element is Light—the good that exists in all beings.

When the crown chakra is in alignment, we'll have direct access to our intelligence, wisdom, and memory banks. If we're walking the spiritual path, we'll feel a strong sense of connection to the Universe and have faith and trust in our higher power.

If there's a lack of energy in this center, there's a good chance we'll feel that life is meaningless or we'll lack a sense of purpose or a reason for being here on the planet.

If you want to bring healing and awareness to this chakra, you are guided to have a clear, open, and vulnerable conversation with your Creator. The crown space helps you move beyond the idea of God/Source/the Universe and into the direct experience of that presence.

VIBE 50
Connecting to life-force

Life-force runs through our veins. It passes through every organ of our body. It flows through the animals and vegetables of the planet. It moves through everything that is. It is powerful, magical, and real. It is our connection to love, to wisdom, to the angels, to healing, and to the Universe.

It is running through you now. You can tap into its beat and wave.

If you have ever seen the movie *Avatar* (and if you haven't, you need to), you will remember that there is a subtle life-force that runs through all of the avatars, their plants, animals, and land. All of this energy is connected to the force of being that they call Eywa. This is similar to what clairvoyants see and to the level of connectivity we can reach when we engage in meditation.

When we meditate and connect to our breath, we create a more conscious connection to the life-force, to what the ancient yogis called *prana*. When we breathe in with the awareness that we are connecting to the subtle life-force pulsing through the Universe, we can "see" this energy in everyone and everything. Our eyes may be open, our eyes may be closed, we may be seeing this energy in our mind, but however we see it, the key is knowing it is there.

Pure divine life-force is moving through every person, every animal, every plant.

It is moving through you now.

VIBE OF THE DAY

Look around you, breathe with awareness, and know that the Universe is alive in you and all beings.

"I inhale, drawing life and energy into my being.

I exhale, connecting to the vision of living prana.

I inhale, awakening to life itself.

I exhale, knowing that all beings are connected.

I inhale, giving thanks for life.

I exhale, knowing that life is giving thanks for me."

VIBE 51
No separation

As you become more spiritually aware, sometimes it's easy to forget about the foundations of your pathway. You are a bright light in the world and the Universe is grateful for you. You are shining and being the positive force in the room, but it's important to remember that you aren't doing this without support.

Nothing in this Universe can be separate. All is One.

You may have encountered loss and the sadness of being physically separate from the people you love. Separation and loss are very real and very painful experiences. But through these experiences, we are led to understand what it feels like to be connected and united. And the truth is that you are here today, working on your recovery and dedicated to experiencing love. This is a miracle.

If you are missing someone, know that they are with you now, connected to and through your heart. If it's someone in heaven, know that you can place your hand on your heart and think of them, and they will feel your love. And if you stay alert, you will also feel theirs.

Even if someone is physically separate
from you, their love is with you.

If you are feeling a loss or missing something, know that this feeling is temporary, or at least it will only dominate your mind for a short time, and through feeling it and connecting to it, you will be able to turn it inside out and experience love and connection once more.

"I am one with the Universe.

It feels so good to know I am never separate.

The love in my heart connects me to all those I love.

*I awaken the memory in my mind that
allows me to feel connected.*

*Thank you, Universe, for helping me realize there is
no time, distance, or space between me and love.*

I am love."

VIBE 52
Spring-clean your aura

Your aura is the field of spiritual energy that projects from your physical body. It is a subtle energy affected by your state of mind, how balanced your chakras are, and the environment to which you are exposed.

You may not realize it, but your aura is always sharing information with you. You know when you walk into a room and feel there's a "weird vibe" or when you're speaking to someone and they absolutely drain you? That's your aura giving you information that the environment or energy you are being exposed to is not in alignment with where you are at or how you want to feel.

Your aura also shares information about you. Many sensitives and clairvoyants are able to see or intuit auras, and often describe them as having a particular color or size.

Auras are subtle energy and therefore impressionable—they are always changing, just like our mood. When we're in a high-vibrational state, our aura is clear and filled with positive energy. When we're in a low-vibrational state, our aura often becomes smaller and "murky," and we might even describe ourselves as feeling "unclear" or "fuzzy." This might be because we've picked up energy that's dragging us down. Also, sometimes people can send negative energy or "the evil eye" our way. We can block this with spiritual practice, but if we don't realize it has happened, it can stay in our aura for a long time.

The higher our vibration, the clearer our aura, and the clearer our aura, the higher our vibration. Therefore it's important to clear our auric field regularly. We can do this through visualization, prayer, meditation, sea-salt baths, and even spending time in nature, especially deep in the forest or by the sea. Why not spring-clean your aura now?

VIBE OF THE DAY

*"Thank you, Universe, for blasting golden
healing light through my aura.*

*Thank you for clearing any lower vibrations, stories, and
negative impressions from my energy field. Thank you for
extracting harsh judgments, psychic attacks, and the evil
eye from my energy. I claim this space as my own.*

I am immersed in universal light.

I am protected by the cosmos.

I am safe in my field.

And so it is."

VIBE 53
Cutting the cords

The world is entangled and connected through invisible bonds, which means we have connections to past situations, relationships, and those we love. These bonds are known as "cords."

There are two types of cords: cords of love and cords of fear.

Cords of love connect us to our loved ones and happy memories, and strengthen our divine connection. They help us physically connect with those we love. How many times have you thought of a loved one and they've called only seconds later?

Cords of fear hold us in the past and can feed our energy with haunting memories that can be traumatic, draining, and damaging. They hold us in repetitive patterns where we keep reliving our own history rather than raising our vibration.

But the Universe has brought you here because it wants you to experience empowerment. This is the lifetime in which you have chosen to heal, grow, and remember who you truly are. Know that you are the keeper of your energy, mind, and body, and with the help of the Universe, you can cut the cords of fear from your energy field and make space for more love, expansiveness, and growth.

Cutting the cords is recommended regularly to ensure that you aren't carrying around any extra energies that are draining you or rooting you in the past. Do it after difficult situations or when you are in a spiral of thinking about your past.

If these cords remain, you will only feed your fears. If they are cut, you will make space for freedom.

VIBE OF THE DAY

The best way to imagine the cords is as strings that are energetically hooked into your body.

"Thank you, Universe, for cutting the unnecessary cords that bind me to people, places, situations, fears, stories, narratives, institutions, limited thinking, old ways of being, pain, trauma, the past, or any other 'stuff' that stands between me and my goodness.

These cords are now being cut, removed, and unplugged by the holiest light beings.

Angels, swirl around me, holding me in a sacred space where it is safe for me to connect with the voice of my soul.

I claim my freedom.

I am safe.

I am free.

And so it is."

VIBE 54

Getting good with Source

There's a good chance that on your spiritual path you've had a few challenging moments with "God." "God" has become a word that puts off many people. They associate the very idea with judgment and torment.

If you're good with "God," then great, you'll swim through this lesson (but please bear with me). If you're not, I'm so glad to have you here. First of all, let's replace the word "God" with "Source."

Next, know that in order to raise your vibration and shine more brightly on your spiritual pathway, it's good to get over any negative ideas you have about the divine. You are encouraged to know that Source, or the Universe, isn't a man, isn't a religion, isn't a dogma, and isn't a set of rules to tell you who, what, or how to be.

The Universe is a presence of love that desires nothing from you. It gives you its full permission to live your life the way you want to live it. It places no expectations on you and there's no punishment coming your way if you don't make it to church or your meditation mat this weekend—absolutely none.

The truth is, if you've been told something about God to make you fearful, it's just someone's way of trying to control you or get you to conform to their way of thinking. It's not real. Only love is real.

VIBE OF THE DAY

"Today I choose to leave behind all fear regarding the divine.

*I lovingly release all false claims, power
trips, traumas, and warnings.*

I am ready to move beyond the limitations of others' dogma.

I realize that the Source of creation is a presence of love.

This presence will do nothing to harm me.

Nor has it punished me in this lifetime.

In every experience I encounter, I have a choice.

Today I choose love. I choose to accept the love of the divine.

*I choose to allow love to be the force that guides me as
I leave behind all that no longer serves me, my spiritual
growth, or my purpose, which is to be happy.*

I am free!

And so it is!"

VIBE 55

Finding reason in the happening

You may have heard the phrase "Everything happens for a reason." You may even have used it, but it can be really difficult to believe it, especially when things are going wrong.

Believing that everything happens for a reason can create the idea that the Universe is punishing you or wanting to teach you a lesson, but it isn't. The Universe is love.

The Universe doesn't send painful situations into your life to teach you a lesson.

The Universe has not punished you in the past.

The Universe wants you to be whole, healed, and free.

But life happens. Everything here in our world is the result of a number of decisions, actions, and non-actions. Every step leads to another step and the step after that.

When things go wrong, it isn't because the Universe has conspired against us, it's because life has unfolded in a particular way, based on all the different factors of environment, choice, health, belief, action, and so on.

It can be easy to want to know *why* something is happening or find the root cause of why something has occurred. But this isn't the best way to raise your vibration. You may never get to the bottom of it, but you can find a new reason for being as a result of whatever you have encountered.

Things may not happen for a reason, but *you can find reason in the happening*.

Raising your vibration isn't about transcending pain or challenges. It's about facing pain and challenges head on and finding a reason to continue on. That's what it means to embody purpose.

You are here for a purpose. You are here because you can help, you can heal, you can help heal!

VIBE OF THE DAY

"My destiny is to heal and share healing with the world.

The Universe is my greatest supporter.

I can find reason in every happening.

Sharing light fills me with purpose."

VIBE 56
Divine experience initiation

When we begin activating the kundalini, it moves up through the chakra system, and by the time it reaches the crown, it is the most potent form of life-force available, for it holds the actualized awareness of all the chakras it has passed through. So the experience of safety, embodiment, focused will, an open heart, full expression, and clear vision becomes available to us.

The crown chakra governs all of our spiritual learning and all of our knowledge. It is essentially always open, but unless we've done the work to align the rest of our energy, its gifts aren't available to us.

The more we study, meditate, and dedicate our awareness to spirituality, though, the more potent and focused the energy of the crown becomes. And the more potent and focused it becomes, the closer we come to experiencing heaven on Earth as a fully embodied light being.

Are you ready to have your very own, full-body visceral experience that not only are you your body and mind, but all of the Universe too?

VIBE OF THE DAY

"I have grown.

I have healed.

I have released the constrictions of my ego and fear.

I was born to remember.

I was born to awaken.

I am willing to have my God experience.

I am willing to remember that I am the Universe.

I am this body and I am so much more.

I am this body and the body of the cosmos.

I am united with light and life.

I am ready for my personal encounter with the Source of creation.

Kundalini, rise, potency, rise, activate my ancient knowing that I have never left the Source I have come from.

I am one with all."

SEED

Seed
(Earth Star)

The Earth Star chakra is found within the body's energy field around 6–12 feet (1.8–3.6m) below ground level, but we can access the tip of its energy from about 12 inches (30cm) below our feet. It is the spiritual anchor that connects us directly with Earth energy. The best way to describe Earth energy is to imagine a giant crystal deep underground to which we can "anchor" ourselves. I often imagine roots growing from the soles of my feet, penetrating the Earth, and winding themselves around a giant crystal that holds me emotionally and energetically on this physical plane of existence.

On an emotional level, the Earth Star is the chakra that represents our connection to Earth, sense of belonging, and capacity to be grounded.

Energetically, it is seen as a copper color. Because it's a fifth-dimensional chakra, it goes beyond the elements of the Earth.

The Earth Star doesn't lack energy, but we can feel disconnected from it if the rest of our chakras aren't in alignment, which will leave us longing for meaning and purpose.

When we bring all our chakras into alignment, we're able to access the Earth Star, which can provide us a deeper sense of meaning and belonging. If you are someone who has often questioned your reason for being here, the Earth Star can hold your spirit like a mother and make you feel welcome on this planet.

When we are connected to the Earth Star, we can connect with information held inside the planet, including elder wisdom, ancestral wisdom, and the angels who are working on the planet.

All of the practices in this section are dedicated to clearing the energies around you so that you can align with the Earth Star, root down into the Earth, and know this is where you are supposed to be.

VIBE 57
I chose to be here

You aren't here by accident—you have chosen to be here. Before you were in this life and in this body, your soul had the opportunity to enter the cycle of life.

You chose to be here on this planet and share the light that you are.

The planet chose to keep you here and is welcoming in your light.

You are here on purpose and for a purpose.

When you remember that you chose to be here, you send deep energetic roots down into the planet and anchor your presence here. You may have tried to escape this lifetime or even your body for a long time, maybe through your habits, your choices, or even your vices, but something forced you to stay and encouraged you to awaken. That was your soul.

VIBE OF THE DAY

"I chose to be here.

The Earth is my home.

I anchor my presence here.

There is a purpose for my life.

There is a purpose in my presence here.

Through every choice I make, I can align with this purpose.

I remember why I am here.

I am here to shine."

VIBE 58
Shifting company

When you begin to raise your vibration, those who aren't in alignment may begin to change, or even leave your life. Don't fight this. Trust in the bigger picture. Just continue to raise your vibration, and those who aren't supposed to travel with you will simply detach themselves.

It's important to mention that not everyone has to be in the same vibrational space as you for a relationship to continue. You'll find there will be friendships and connections that stay, even if you evolve to a different space—and there are huge opportunities there too. Let these people continue to be anchors and rocks that keep you grounded, and do the same for them.

When you ascend in vibration, it's important to stay centered toward your relationships. Don't force anyone to change who they are or invite them to match your frequency. Moreover, begin to see them through the most holy and loving eyes, accepting them for who they are and where they are—that's what being at a high vibration is all about.

For tumultuous relationships, think of yourself as a tree. During fall, in order to survive through the cold of winter, a tree simply lets go of everything that is dragging it down. Then, no matter what comes toward it or what uncertainty it faces, through the resilience of its being it will continue to grow.

So, trust in the changes that are unfolding around you. Let the old foliage go and you'll continue to grow.

VIBE OF THE DAY

"When I raise my vibration, I upgrade my experience of life.

*I release the energies that hold me back
and make way for the new.*

I attract relationships that reflect the truth of who I am.

I am surrounded by those who inspire me and those I can inspire.

My life is filled with goodness."

VIBE 59

Your energy is more important than manners

Your energy is *your* energy—don't let anyone or anything get in the way of feeling good.

When someone or something is making you uncomfortable, it's a clear message from your intuition to back away, get out, or even leave.

Energy speaks volumes.

If you're hearing it's time to go, then it's time to go. This information is protecting you from harm (or further harm).

Worried that it would be impolite to leave? Your energy is more important than manners. Of course, if you can find a way to excuse yourself from a situation that is making you feel uncomfortable, then do so, but don't wait for permission from anyone to leave a space that is making you feel unsettled or unbalanced. Instead, let this be an opportunity for self-empowerment.

When you listen to these clear signals from your body and act upon them, you strengthen your spiritual abilities to know and heal. These messages are guidance that will help you live in the highest vibration.

VIBE OF THE DAY

"When my energy speaks, I listen.
I follow the subtle messages of my intuition.
I follow the guidance of my soul.
Following the signals within keeps me safe.
The Universe protects me."

VIBE 60
Clear your world, clear your energy

When it comes to your world, everything within it represents your vibration in physical form. Therefore, if your world has a lot of clutter in it, there's a good chance that your energy will have too. Physical clutter equals psychic clutter, and when there's psychic clutter, the outer expression of your life will feel messy, all over the place, and lack order.

Have you ever noticed that the person with the cluttered car is always running late? That the people with cluttered bedrooms are all over the place? That an untidy desk or workspace indicates a flaky, unorganized, and unprepared colleague?

That goes for the opposite end of the spectrum too—when there's too much order in your world, there's a good chance you'll feel stiff and restricted and will find it difficult to get into the flow of life. The ideal is a happy medium.

Often when we have clutter in our life, we feel that we haven't got time to clear it, but on an energetic level, we realize that through taking the time to clear the clutter, we are in fact creating more time and space for completion in our world.

VIBE OF THE DAY

Today you are encouraged to find the parts of your world that are holding clutter—maybe your desk or your wardrobe, or even your friends group! Take the time to release the old energies from your space, for by doing so, you are creating more room for order, clarity, and growth.

"Releasing physical clutter clears energetic space.
I release the old from my life and create room for the new.
When I let go, I create space for growth."

VIBE 61
I am home (Earth Star activation)

You are a spiritual being incarnated in a human shell, so there's a good chance that for a lot of your life you've felt out of place or had a longing for "home."

It makes sense, because before you were here in physical form, you were a boundless being, dancing across the sky among the stars. In fact, you were a star yourself.

But you were called to the Earth and you chose to accept this incarnation and the many others that you have lived before this lifetime.

This lifetime is different, though, because you're remembering that even though you are in a body, you are so much more. You are realizing that everything you have been searching for is within you, including that sense of "home." For you have never left the energy you have come from.

The Earth Star chakra is the energy that anchors you to the Earth. This center is similar to a memory card inside a computer: it holds all of the Earth's lessons, including her capacity to cope in times of stress, to survive, and even to heal.

You can access this energy—it's available to you now and it comes through knowing that you are where you are supposed to be: *home*.

All you have been searching for is within you now.

Wherever you are, you are home,
because you are the Universe.

"I am at home on Earth because I am at home within myself.

It is not my duty to know every facet of my journey here on Earth.

This lifetime is an opportunity to trust.

I trust that I am where I am supposed to be.

I anchor into the Earth and know that I am home."

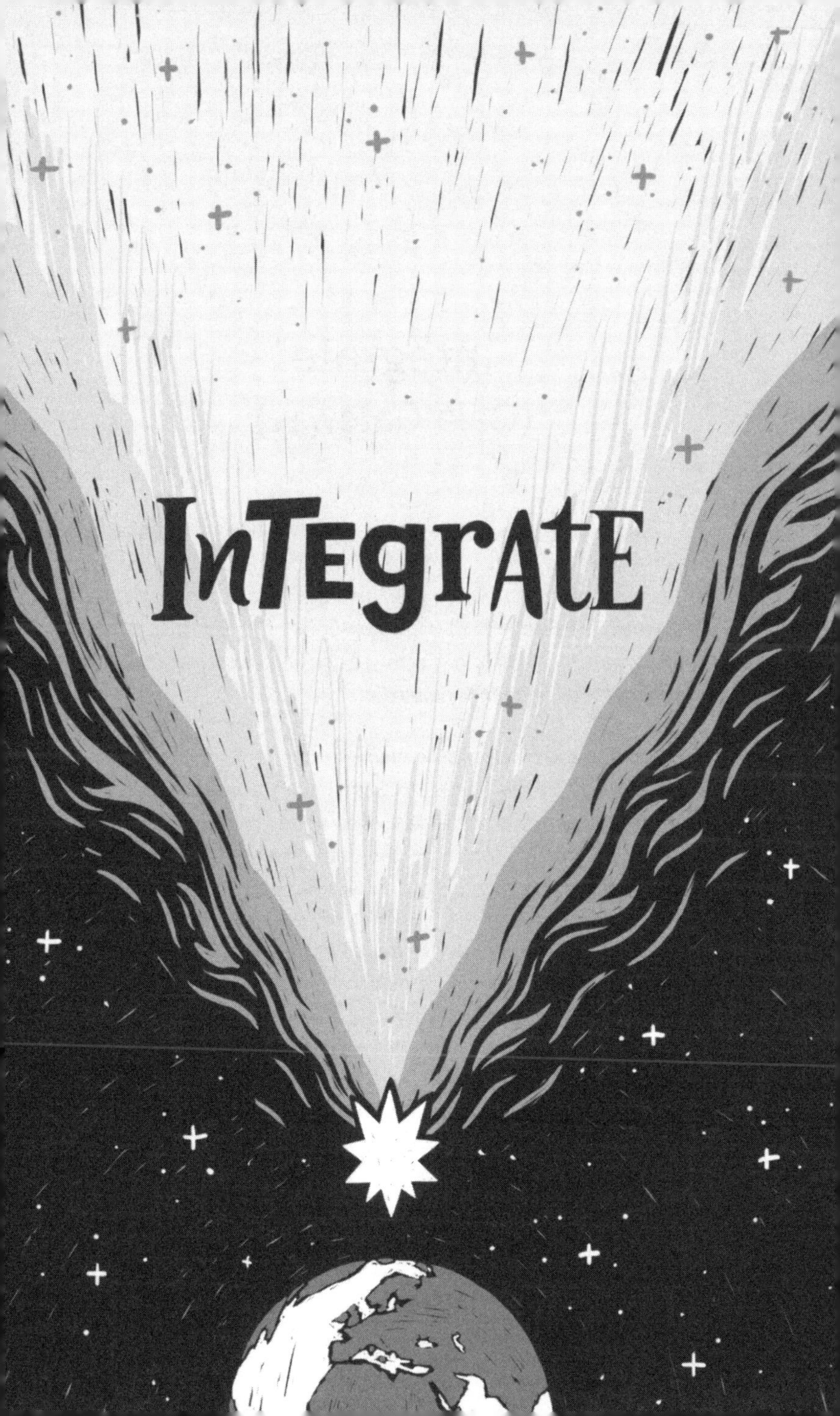
InTegrAtE

Integrate
(Gaia Gateway)

The Gaia Gateway is a gateway of energy held beyond the physical dimension at the center of the Earth. On an energetic level, we can gain access to it through the Earth Star chakra. It connects to Gaia, which is essentially the holy spirit of Mother Earth, and helps us align with the Matrix of Earthly Consciousness—basically the energy that the kundalini was birthed from.

The Gaia Gateway helps us reclaim our right to remember our divine mission on the planet. In this space we are not only able to connect to our own soul's past lives upon Earth, but also to all of the primordial wisdom that has been held in the Earth since her conception.

In a way, the Gaia Gateway is similar to the Alice in Wonderland rabbit-hole, for it connects us to another space, in this case the "inner Earth" that shamans often call "the underworld." This isn't to be considered a "dark" place, for it's where the divine wisdom of the Great Mother is held and where we can be reborn and reclaim the aspects of our power that have been lying dormant.

Those who work with plant medicine or go on shamanic journeys will know this space. It can feel like a completely different world, beyond life and death. It's where we are able to face our greatest fears, overcome darkness, and emerge immersed in light. It is the womb of the Earth.

Gaining access to the Gaia Gateway doesn't have to happen via shamanic journeys or even meditation; it's a matrix of consciousness that streams into our being with information that will support our evolution. I think of it as offering downloads of Earthly wisdom that remind us of our reason for being here.

All of the lessons in this section are dedicated to aligning with the energies of the Gaia Gateway.

VIBE 62

Healing myself heals my lineage

You come from a long line of souls.

For hundreds and maybe even thousands of years, all those who have been part of your family line have prayed for healing, prayed for change, prayed for a better way.

You were born in response to those prayers.

The fact that you are living this life, walking the spiritual path, and working on raising your vibration means that you have heard the divine call to bring healing to your lineage.

You chose your family line. You chose your parents.

You didn't choose the traumas, but you chose to heal them.

Whatever you have faced, whatever you have endured can end with you.

> ***You are here to change the narrative***
> ***and change the karma.***

Know that all that you heal in yourself reaches deep into the roots of all those who have gone before you. Know that healing yourself is creating new pathways, new opportunities, and prosperity for those to come.

Let your legacy be healing your lineage.

VIBE OF THE DAY

"My life is the answered prayer of my ancestors.

I live for my lineage.

All that I heal in myself is healing for my family line.

My life is a demonstration of what is possible.

*All that I heal in myself creates new opportunities
for the generations that will follow.*

My life is healing.

I accept this mission."

VIBE 63
Old stories

When we choose to live a spiritual life, we choose to embody healing.

Along the way, there will be many opportunities to experience healing. Every facet of our life will become an opportunity to embody love.

Our patience will be tested at times, but when we take a moment to reflect, we will realize we have come a long way. Take that moment now. During the hardships, you may have felt you didn't have it in you to carry on, and you may even have given up, but you are here today. Why?

Your soul is tenacious. It never gives up.

This is important because on your pathway to embodying healing, you're going to encounter old stories—aspects of your life that you thought were healed and done with. This can feel alarming and at times overwhelming, but it doesn't need to.

Often when an old situation reappears, it's an opportunity to reflect. These old parts of our life are showing up as milestone markers, helping us realize how far we've come and how deeply we've healed.

Think about it. You're not where you were, are you? You're not who you were. You're not those old stories.

Stay composed. Don't get pulled in. It's like meeting that old high-school bully in the street a decade later. They don't know the damage they caused; they probably don't even remember. Smile and walk on by.

VIBE OF THE DAY

"When old stories revisit my life, it's an opportunity to see how far I've come.

When an old wound is reopened, it's an opportunity for light to reach deeper within.

I let the light in.

I am healed, soul deep."

223

VIBE 64
Karma clearing

Do you ever feel that there's a part of your life that you just can't seem to get sorted? You know, an aspect of your life that is continuously difficult and you've never been able to put your finger on why?

There's a good chance it's a karmic lesson from beyond this lifetime.

This isn't the first time you have walked the Earth. You have had many opportunities to be human. Sometimes, when a life lesson has been challenging in a previous incarnation, we are reborn still trying to heal it, and thus we experience karmic blockages.

When I speak about a "previous incarnation," it could be a life before this life or even earlier in this life. But wherever a karmic block comes from, you can ask for it to be removed.

The Universe has the ability to clear blockages from our life, especially when our current incarnation is geared toward making this planet a better place. We can choose what we carry with us, and if we're carrying something that we don't want and that doesn't even relate to this lifetime, of course we can have it removed.

Just through knowing this is an option, I hope you are feeling relieved.

"Divine Universe, wheel of karma,

Thank you for releasing all the threads of energy that stand between me and my freedom. Thank you for clearing all karmic bonds that bind me to lessons of previous incarnations and aspects of who I used to be.

I now clear, cancel, and release all karmic bonds and fear memories from my vibration.

I claim my divine right to be free.

And so it is."

VIBE 65

The Earth holds the answer

When you start learning about the Universe, there's a tendency to send your requests "up" into the sky. This is because for a long time, through mainstream religion and media, we've learned that the divine is high and unreachable, but it is also beneath us, in the Earth.

Great Mother Earth has been here for around 4.3 billion years, with physical life existing on her for around 3.7 billion of those, so I'm sure you'll find it safe to agree that she's lived a long time. And she's lived through it all—evolution, expansion, disaster, and war. She's lived, she's lost, she's grown and evolved. All of this learning and growing, all of this knowledge and wisdom, is held deep within her.

The Earth has a spirit, a presence—spiritual energy that is available to you now. Just as you can develop the capacity to tune in to the Universe, so you can develop the capacity to hear the Great Mother.

If you require information or insight and you're just not able to receive it, maybe it's because you've been looking up for the answer when the whole time it's been at your feet.

VIBE OF THE DAY

Go for a walk in nature, let the soles of your feet kiss the ground, and ask the Earth for guidance.

"Mother Earth, thank you for giving me a planet to call home.

I am so grateful to be connected to you.

Thank you for imparting your knowledge and wisdom to me.

I am willing to listen to your insights and guidance.

I let your spirit lead the way on my path.

And so it is."

VIBE 66

Calling back your power
(Gaia Gateway activation)

You have a divine right to be here.

You have spent lifetimes upon lifetimes preparing for where you are today.

Every lesson, every challenge, every wound that you have healed has led you to this point.

You could have chosen to live your life without thought and awareness, but you didn't. You chose to answer the call to connect to something greater. You chose to remember your true self.

Just by choosing to live from the highest vibration possible, you have given your life meaning. Just by being on this planet, you have made it a safer, brighter, and more loving place to be.

During your journey to this moment, you have faced challenges, experienced fear, and endured loss. During those moments of darkness, there's a good chance that you have left small fragments of your soul behind. Or lost sight of yourself and felt your power being stripped from you.

All of this can be called back.

The Gaia Gateway is the portal to the Earth's primeval consciousness. When we call back all the fragments of ourselves from this lifetime and the many lifetimes before, we give permission for our Gaia

Gateway to be activated, and when we do so, we know that we have every right to be here.

"Thank you, Great Mother Earth.

*For holding sacred space for me to
reclaim the lost parts of myself.*

*I call back the fragments of my soul that I have left behind
in this lifetime and any other lifetimes I have lived.*

I reclaim what is truly mine.

My soul is whole.

The Earth is my home.

And so it is."

Activate
(Soul Star)

The Soul Star chakra is found within the body's energy field around 6–12 feet (1.8–3.6m) above the head, but we can access the tip of its energy anywhere from 6 to 12 inches (15–30cm) above the head. It's the spiritual portal that connects us with divine wisdom, our anchor point to the spiritual realms, allowing us to connect with our guides, angels, and soul contracts. The Soul Star is the heavenly sibling to the Earth Star, and connecting to it energetically unlocks information from previous incarnations and the intentions that our soul created before incarnating into this life.

When we bring all of our chakras into alignment and raise our vibration, we have access to the energies and information that are held within the Soul Star. If you've had a spiritual awakening and suddenly felt connected to spiritual guides or angels, for example, you've accessed your Soul Star.

Energetically, the Soul Star is imagined as a star-bright portal that is deep magenta to some and diamond or crystalline to others. It never lacks energy, but we can become disconnected from it. When we do the work related to the main chakras, particularly the brow and crown, however, the natural progression is to unlock the energies held in the Soul Star and commune with high elders, angels, and divine masters of ancient wisdom.

All of the lessons in this section are dedicated to aligning with the Soul Star.

VIBE 67
I am willing to be seen

You are like a seed in soul form.

This isn't your first trip to Earth and it probably won't be your last.

Many lifetimes have prepared you for this one.

You were born to bloom.

**You were born to grow, expand, and
show the beauty you hold within.**

You may feel like a flower that has been cut from its stem and removed from the soil it calls home. But all this may happen to a flower and it may still find a way to unfurl its petals and bloom.

You are similar. You may not always find yourself in a place that feels comfortable. At some time in your life, you are sure to find yourself in wide-open spaces that make you feel vulnerable.

But it's in your vulnerability that your safety lies, for in that moment your shields drop and you reveal the essence of your beauty, and all those around you feel called to reveal themselves as well.

It is your nature to unfold, unfurl, and bloom.

And if you don't do it in this lifetime, you'll have to do it in the next.

So, bloom. Be seen. In all of your glory.

VIBE OF THE DAY

"I am willing to be seen.

I let myself unfurl.

I am willing to bloom,
to reveal my whole self, soul deep.

When I allow myself to be seen,
I reveal the tender parts of my soul that
can never be tarnished or broken,
for my true self is whole, healed, and complete.

My true self is unborn and therefore can never die.

I am willing to be seen."

VIBE 68
Do not fear the dark

Mainstream media and religion have capitalized on humans being scared of the dark and the idea of darkness. But darkness isn't evil, it's simply uncertainty—it presents the opportunity to experience the unknown.

Darkness is a huge part of who you are as a human. In fact, during the nine months your mother held you in her belly, you were in darkness, and look how you turned out! Furthermore, in order for your human body to rejuvenate, you have to close your eyes and trust in the darkness in order to sleep.

When things go dark, we can of course get scared and overwhelmed, for we live in a physical world that thrives on control, but when darkness appears, know that it is an opportunity, or even an assignment, to step into trust.

You aren't supposed to know everything that is unfolding; your duty is to trust in the Universe that created you and is within you.

If you look up into the midnight sky, you'll see that without darkness, the stars cannot shine. You are a star in its next form, therefore it's important you remember that whenever darkness appears, it's presenting the perfect holding space for your light to be seen and recognized.

You are a great light, and that light will never go out. Whenever you face darkness or uncertainty, it has the opportunity to shine.

Call up this great light from within and let it show the way.

"Whenever darkness appears, my light has the opportunity to shine. Whenever I step into uncertainty, I have the opportunity to trust. Thank you, Universe, for holding space for me to shine."

VIBE 69
Calling all angels

You have a guardian angel who has been with you from the moment you chose to come to Earth. This being of pure white light will be with you until you return to the heart of the Universe.

Angels are the heartbeats of the Universe. As far as I'm concerned, they are extensions of universal love coming to us in personal form. Our relationship with our guardian angel reflects our relationship with the universal life-force.

Angels don't want us to bow down to them, they just want us to experience peace and happiness on Earth.

Angels respond to our prayers and thoughts, and I have learned that they *love* to be thanked—not because they enjoy the praise or the feeling of being powerful, but because when we thank them, the gratitude we feel creates miracles in our life.

Your angel loves you unconditionally and honors your free will and will never override it unless it is a life-or-death situation. So the only way you'll be able to experience your angel is by accepting that they are close to you and inviting them into your life. Invite them in today!

VIBE OF THE DAY

"Hello, guardian angel!

*It's so good to know you are here with me
now and looking after me and my life.*

I am so grateful that I have your support.

I open myself up to your presence and your help.

*Thank you for reminding me of your presence, for sending
me signs, and for revealing to me what I need to know.*

Thank you, thank you, thank you!"

VIBE 70
Living with purpose

When we think of living with purpose, it can be very easy to start thinking about those we look up to and those who are making dramatic improvements in the world, and then compare them to ourselves.

But living with purpose isn't something that can be measured. The Universe doesn't have angels with clipboards making notes! So, don't let your ego run away with the idea that you aren't living your purpose. Whenever you feel that you aren't doing enough, or fall into a state of comparison, your ego is running the show.

The Universe appreciates that every small change contributes to a huge change.

All things done with love are purposeful.

So, step away from comparison, step away from measuring your progress, and focus on being the loving being that you are.

Your life and your purpose are unique to you. Trust that all that you're doing and all that you're striving for are making a difference.

That's what it means to be high vibration.

VIBE OF THE DAY

"I surrender my need to compare.

I release my concerns around purpose.

Every small change contributes to healing.

When I set the intention to share love, I am living with purpose.

When I step into self-care, I am living with purpose.

When I intend to be of service, I am living with purpose.

I am living with purpose."

VIBE 71

I am Heaven on Earth
(Soul Star activation)

You are where you are supposed to be. Where you are is where your light is required.

It may be a challenging situation. When we begin to walk the path of light, our ego may convince us that it's supposed to be perfect and easy, but that's not true. It's called spiritual *work* because it takes work. That's why the high-vibrational path is the path less traveled, because not everyone is ready to do the work.

Many receive wake-up calls, but choose to carry on as normal. You did not. You chose to awaken. Therefore, every challenge you are facing, every aspect of repression and resistance that you are facing, is an assignment and an opportunity for you to act with purpose. You are here to contribute to the healing of the world, and you do that by healing *your* world.

Of course, there are going to be aspects of your world that you cannot change personally, but the more challenges you are presented with, the greater your opportunities to let your love out into the world.

The Soul Star chakra is a guiding light that becomes available to you when you let your love reach those parts of your world you have never reached before. This energy center contains all the wisdom of your soul that has come down through lifetimes and lifetimes, and this will give you the courage and strength to continue on.

VIBE OF THE DAY

"I let my love reach where it has never reached before.

I open up to the ancient wisdom of my soul.

*I let the light of all my previous incarnations guide me,
for I was born to be who I am today.*

I was born to be a light."

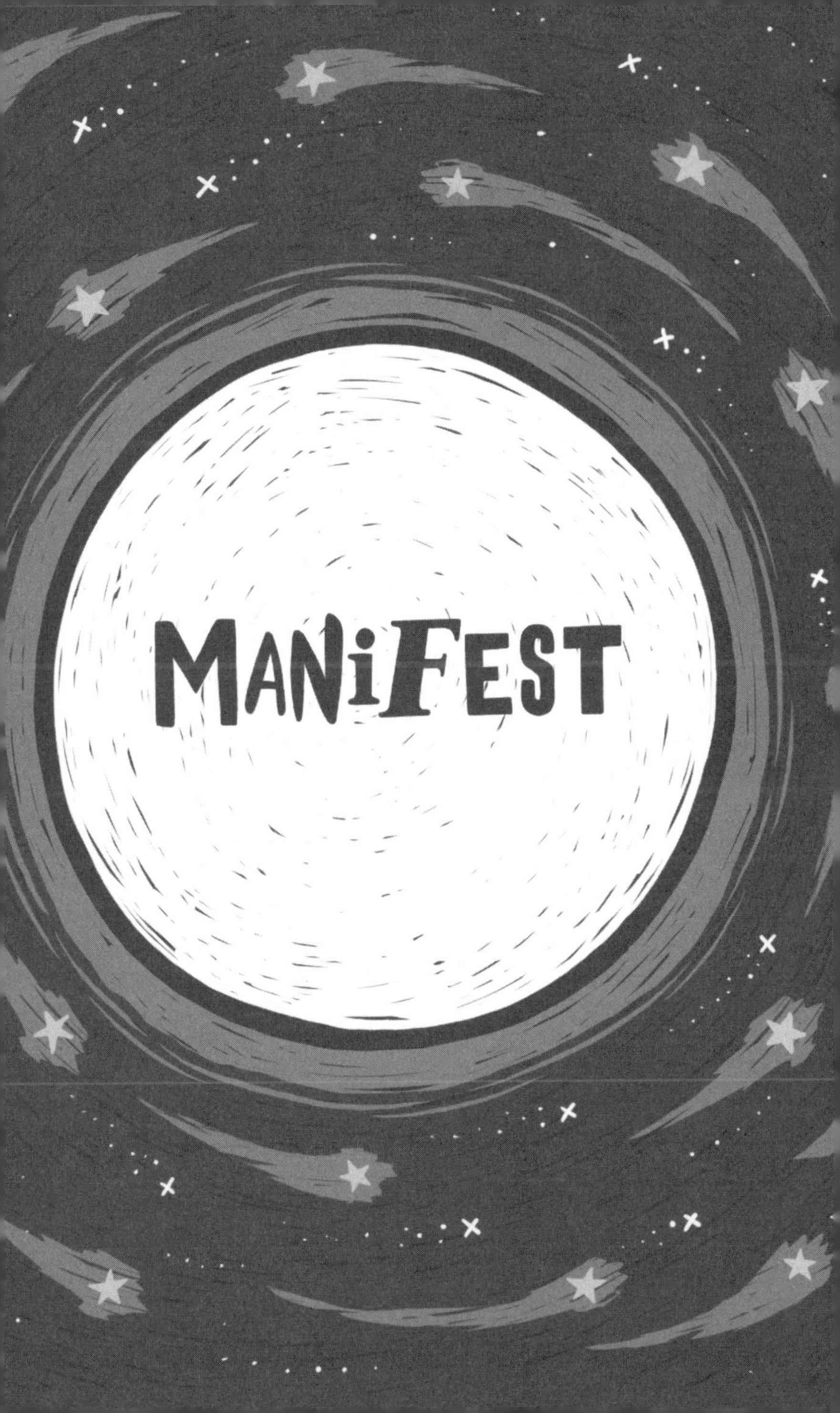
MANIFEST

Manifest
(Stellar Gateway)

The Stellar Gateway is a gateway of energy held beyond the physical dimension at the center of the Universe. On an energetic level, we gain access to it through all of the other chakras. This portal connects us to the energy of creation, which essentially takes all of our intentions from our current life and pre-incarnation and writes them into the creation of our life.

So the Stellar Gateway is a higher-dimensional space like a vortex that curates our experience upon planet Earth and holds all of the information about our existence. It can help us remember our cosmic origin and it allows us to connect directly with "the God particle."

This chakra reminds me of the TV show Stargate, for it's like a pool of energy that bridges all of the realms, and through it, instead of knowing about God, we have a direct experience of that presence. I believe that when people who have had a near-death experience recall moving through a tunnel of light, they are recalling moving through the Stellar Gateway, through the wormhole between heaven, Earth, and beyond.

Accessing the Stellar Gateway, just like the Gaia Gateway, is a spontaneous occurrence based on all of the other spiritual work we do. It is through the raising of our vibration, the alignment of our chakras, and the ascent of our kundalini, that we are given access to information and support that go beyond human comprehension.

When we speak about "cosmic ordering" or "manifestation," it's the energy of our thoughts pulling the energy of creation through the Stellar Gateway so that what we have envisaged on a mental level comes into the physical. So, the Stellar Gateway is what the teachings of Abraham-Hicks call "the Vortex" and what scientists call "the quantum field."

All of the lessons in this section are dedicated to accessing and creating with the Stellar Gateway.

VIBE 72
Creating space to allow

It's your destiny to experience good things because your essence is goodness. When good things aren't occurring, space is required for them to enter. There's so much information out there regarding manifesting and creating your dreams—so much so that we feel we're not doing enough, and often keep checking back in with the Universe to make sure our prayers have been heard.

It's important to remember that it's not your role to micromanage the Universe. If your intentions are clear and the action steps you have taken are coming with ease, then the next step is to allow.

When you create space, you let things unfold as they need to. It's a symbol of your trust in the power that's within you and the power that created you.

You have the ability to manifest miracles in your life. Get out of the Universe's way and let it support you.

> **Don't go looking for a miracle. Know that it is already in place.**
>
> **When you allow it, you'll see it.**

You can create miracles, but you cannot direct them. Leave that to the Universe.

VIBE OF THE DAY

You are encouraged to create space in your mind for the seeds of your dreams to grow. When you plant a seed in the garden, you don't dig it up to see if it's growing or not, you expect it to grow. So, trust in the Universe. Know that whatever intentions you have put out into the field have been heard and that the wheels of the Universe are turning for your highest good.

"Dear Universe,

I hand this over to you.

Thank you for placing your hands of light upon this situation.

And everyone and everything involved.

I let go.

I create space for miracles.

I know miraculous energy is here now.

I allow miracles to be revealed.

And so it is."

VIBE 73

The miraculous mind

The only thing you can do wrong when manifesting is to fall into doubt and fear. But you can overcome this by turning on your miraculous mind.

Your miraculous mind is the aspect of you that moves into the totality of possibility, trusting that anything can happen, no matter its size or likelihood, or how uncanny it would be if it did take place. The Universe is a miraculous place, remember, and you deserve to bring even more miracles into your life.

The miraculous mind is about trust, and at times expectation, also sharing, service, and dedication. It isn't about materialism, it's about enjoying the nice things in life while remaining open to both success and what the world would call "failure."

With miraculous thinking, when something doesn't go "to plan," you trust that your thinking, energy, and ability to align with the Universe are still bringing about the most amazing shifts in your life.

The miraculous mind overcomes the doubt-and-fear mind. It knows there is an amazing shift occurring in the here and now.

*"I am one with the cosmos,
living within the totality of possibility.*

I trust that anything is possible.

Miracles occur naturally as I focus on plenty in my mind.

I am filled with universal potential, supported, and guided."

VIBE 74

I was born to prosper

Prosperity is more than just material and financial wellbeing, it's the energy of being full until you are overflowing.

You were born to be prosperous, because your spirit is full and overflowing.

Prosperity is your inheritance, because where you come from is a realm that was unborn and is therefore undying. It is an energy that will never cease to be.

Your life isn't one small lifetime, it is many, and this is the lifetime in which you are destined to live in a way that your cup of life and light is overflowing.

You were born to prosper.

You were born to prosper in wellbeing and in healing.

You were born to prosper in connections and relationships.

You were born to prosper in opportunities and creativity.

You have come from the heart of the Universe, the divine matrix, the space that has a never-ending capacity to create.

VIBE OF THE DAY

If you are ready to prosper, claim it now.

"I am prosperous because I am spirit embodied.

*I have come from a divine matrix of creativity,
a space that has no beginning and no end.*

My vibration aligns with the consciousness of prosperity.

*I let my life become a living prayer and
demonstration that all things are possible.*

*Thank you, Universe, for filling up the cup
of my heart until I am overflowing.*

I claim my truth: that I was born to prosper in all areas of my life."

VIBE 75

*My most authentic self is
a gift to the world*

In a world that is full of people trying to be someone else, the greatest gift you can give is your most authentic self.

All of your lifetimes and all of the lessons of this lifetime have led you to where you are now. It has taken courage, determination, tenacity, and strength to be who you are today. There have been many times it would have been easier to run away, and you may even have done it, but here you are today in a space of bravery and trust.

Just by being yourself, your whole self, you are living with purpose. By choosing to live your truth, you are allowing healing energy to penetrate deep into the lineage that you were born into and to reach far into the future, preparing the way for coming generations.

Many who have walked the path before you have felt stifled and restrained. You are the living answer to their prayers. By living fully and authentically, you are bringing meaning and purpose to their lifetimes.

Take time to be grateful for those who have gone before you, for they have prepared the way. Know that ancestors and angels are cheering you on as you step into the most authentic version of yourself. And as you reveal the tender and vulnerable aspects of yourself to the world, remember that the only shield you need is your spirit—the part of you that can never be broken or tarnished.

VIBE OF THE DAY

"It is safe for me to be myself.

I am spirit embodied.

I am heaven. I am Earth.

Sharing my truth is my greatest gift to the world."

VIBE 76
Connections

The entire Universe is connected. Everything that was, is, and ever will be is connected through an invisible bond of energy that unites every living being, past, present, and even future.

This information is not new. It has been around for millennia and has been shared by some of the greatest masters to walk the Earth. Modern-day quantum physics is now starting to support it.

The best way to think of the Universe and all its dimensions is like a lattice. All souls and lives are points on this grid. Through it, you are connected to those on the far side of the Earth and they are connected to you. You are connected to all of your ancestors and all of your loved ones. You are connected to all of the different aspects of yourself in the past, present, and future, as well as to all the great minds who were, are, and ever will be.

Therefore, everything that you do for yourself you are doing for the world.

When you remember who you are and that you have come from the stars to be embodied, you access the energies of heaven and Earth and activate the Stellar Gateway chakra. Then all the ancient knowledge and intelligence that will support your journey will be made available to you.

It's your destiny to know and remember.

VIBE OF THE DAY

"I am one with all that is.

Breathing, moving, expressing, and receiving.

I inhale bliss, eternal prana, the energy of the cosmos.

As I exhale, I share this divine essence with the
physical and non-physical dimensions around me.

I feel the Universe within, sparking my eternal fire.

The divine power to change and create is
alive in me, ready to be shared.

I am a star shining in the galaxy of being.

This is my time to light up the Universe, because that is who I am:

I am the Universe."

VIBE 77
Magnetic aura activation

Your aura is the energetic expression of your mental, emotional, physical, and spiritual bodies. It is the electromagnetic field of energy that is projected from the core of your being. It's a living field that is fed nutrients through the activation of your chakras and the raising of your kundalini.

In most healthy humans, this energy is projected 5–6ft (c.1.5m) in all directions, and if you are spiritually centered, it can be projected even further, allowing your presence, light, and purpose to be carried further and wider.

Your aura is the download of information that others experience when you walk into a room, or they see you in a photograph, or even on a video call. It's what allows them to perceive you and the light you carry. It's also the energetic space in which you carry your karma, stories, ideas, and everything that has led you to be who you are today.

The consistency of your aura is similar to that of a spider's web. It's like a grid and it's sticky—it holds onto information, and that's not always good, but it's something that will begin to change as you vibrate on a higher level.

When you consistently step into spiritual practice, embodying the energy of love, service, devotion, and authenticity, the old stagnant energy in your auric field is released into the ether, where it is transformed into neutral energy, creating space for you to emit radiance.

When your aura emits radiance, its consistency shifts from web-like to magnetic, and it draws other radiant energies toward you. Golden opportunities, loving experiences, and living with purpose become your reality.

Right now your aura is radiating a rainbow light—it's bright and clear, for the inner work you have been doing and the purpose you have been curating are now beginning to shine from the inside out. Bathe in the brilliance of who you are and let it be a magnet for miracles in your world.

VIBE OF THE DAY

"The past is the past.

The old is the old.

I release and let go.

Renewed and new,
I allow purpose to unfold.

My aura, shining healthy and bright,
is a magnet to the presence of light.

Miracles around me,
I am safe and free.

I am infinite.

For eternity."

DECLARATION OF LIGHT

A declaration is a formal statement. When made in an affirmative style, it has the capacity to lift our energy and empower our spiritual gifts.

You can make this declaration anytime you need to be inspired to live at the highest vibration.

When you make it, you awaken your light body, or what is called the Merkaba in many ancient teachings.

Mer-ka-ba and *Merkabah* are ancient Egyptian and Hebrew words relating to the ascension process of the soul (rising to the highest vibration). The Hebrew *Merkabah* or *Merkavah* means "chariot" or "vehicle," and it's most commonly associated with the prophet Ezekiel's vision of angels traveling on or in spheres of light. In ancient Egyptian, *mer* means "light," *ka* means "spirit," and *ba* means "body." When these three words are put together, the idea is that light engulfs the spirit and body and there is an opportunity to rise up.

The Merkaba is said to be in the form of a star tetrahedron, an eight-pointed star made from two triangular pyramids, one pointing up and the other pointing down. This is the three-dimensional extension of the hexagram, a symbol that is strongly associated with the Hebrew and Egyptian Mystery schools.

The Merkaba

Within spiritual circles, it is said that we can activate the Merkaba for the ascension process and that when we're aligned on a spiritual level, the star tetrahedron spins at great speed, creating a sphere of unbreakable light around us. This sphere of light can help us move between the dimensions. While we are having a human experience, it creates a portal into the heart of the Universe so that we can connect with guidance and walk the path of light.

The activation of the Merkaba light body is the missing element in a lot of spiritual teachings. It's what the alignment of the chakras and ascent of the kundalini are leading toward. I believe it's the one thing that the many ancient yogis knew about but withheld from the uninitiated, most likely because in ancient times, when the light body was activated, many ascended beyond the human realm.

I know that the Merkaba energy has adapted to the current times, and this light energy is what is required on Earth now, to lead us into a more conscious state of being.

That is why you are here. That is why you have chosen to raise your vibration, to embody the light, and to create a direct link between heaven and Earth.

So, make the declaration of light, and when you have finished, take some time to feel your light body being activated. Visualize a star tetrahedron spinning around your body, creating a force-field of light, a portal between this realm and the next, the experience of heaven on Earth...

MER-KA-BA ACTIVATION
Declaration

"I accept that there is a greater purpose to my life.

*I remember that within me there is a divine
spark of light that will never cease to be.*

I choose to accept that I am soul embodied.

*My being is resilient, strong, and guided, for
I am united with the Source of creation.*

*I am supported by angelic beings and connected to the
minds of masters who walked this path before me.*

I step onto the path of light.

I contribute healing and light to the world.

I am a light.

I am the light.

I am light.

I activate the light of heaven and Earth within my being.

As above, so below.

As within, so without."

The light the Earth has been seeking has arrived.

That light is you.

Thank you for being that light.

And so it is.

Bob Rafferty

ABOUT THE AUTHOR

Kyle Gray has had spiritual encounters from an early age. When he was just four years old, his grandmother's soul visited him from the other side.

Growing up, Kyle always had an ability to hear, feel and see what goes beyond the natural senses, which eventually led him to discover the power of angels and spiritual energy in his teens.

Now Kyle is one of the world's leading angel experts who dedicates his life to helping others discover their spiritual abilities. With his sharp wit, need for truth, and remarkable intuitive gifts, he has become one of the most sought-after teachers within his field and speaks to sell-out crowds across the globe. Kyle believes that spiritual connection is possible for everyone, and he's dedicated to helping people shift their energy and deepen their relationship with the Divine.

Kyle is based in Glasgow, Scotland, and he is a senior yoga teacher with Yoga Alliance Professionals. Kyle teaches through online training courses and Angel Team Community, and is the best-selling author of eight books and the co-creator of five oracle card decks.

f kylegrayuk

@kylegrayuk

@kylegrayuk

www.kylegray.co.uk

www.raiseyourvibration.com

Hay House Podcasts
Bring Fresh, Free Inspiration Each Week!

Hay House proudly offers a selection of life-changing audio content via our most popular podcasts!

Hay House Meditations Podcast

Features your favorite Hay House authors guiding you through meditations designed to help you relax and rejuvenate. Take their words into your soul and cruise through the week!

Dr. Wayne W. Dyer Podcast

Discover the timeless wisdom of Dr. Wayne W. Dyer, world-renowned spiritual teacher and affectionately known as "the father of motivation." Each week brings some of the best selections from the 10-year span of Dr. Dyer's talk show on Hay House Radio.

Hay House Podcast

Enjoy a selection of insightful and inspiring lectures from Hay House Live events, listen to some of the best moments from previous Hay House Radio episodes, and tune in for exclusive interviews and behind-the-scenes audio segments featuring leading experts in the fields of alternative health, self-development, intuitive medicine, success, and more! Get motivated to live your best life possible by subscribing to the free Hay House Podcast.

Find Hay House podcasts on iTunes, or visit www.HayHouse.com/podcasts for more info.

CONNECT WITH

HAY HOUSE

ONLINE

🌐 hayhouse.co.uk   **f** @hayhouse

📷 @hayhouseuk   🐦 @hayhouseuk

▶ @hayhouseuk   ♪ @hayhouseuk

Find out all about our latest books & card decks • Be the first to know about exclusive discounts • Interact with our authors in live broadcasts • Celebrate the cycle of the seasons with us • Watch free videos from your favourite authors • Connect with like-minded souls

'The gateways to wisdom and knowledge are always open.'

Louise Hay